OWLS

Coloring Book for Kids

Blue Wave Press

This book belongs to:

Sample Page Previews

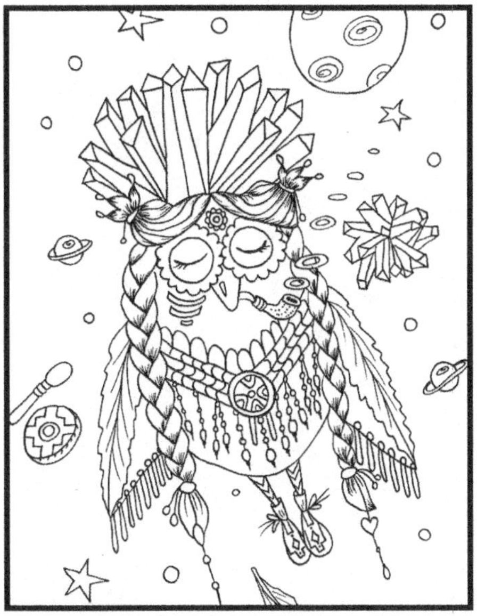
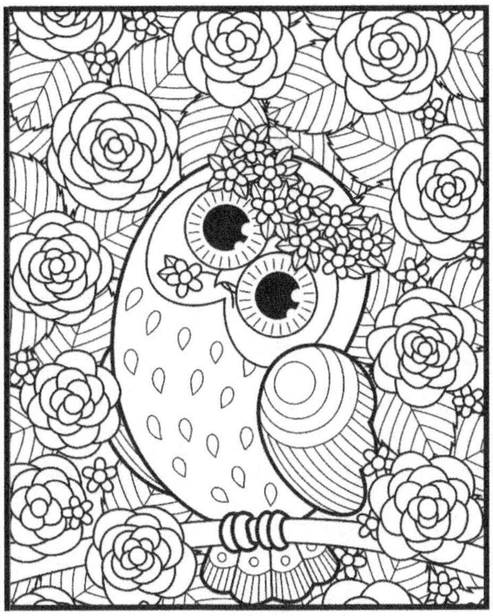
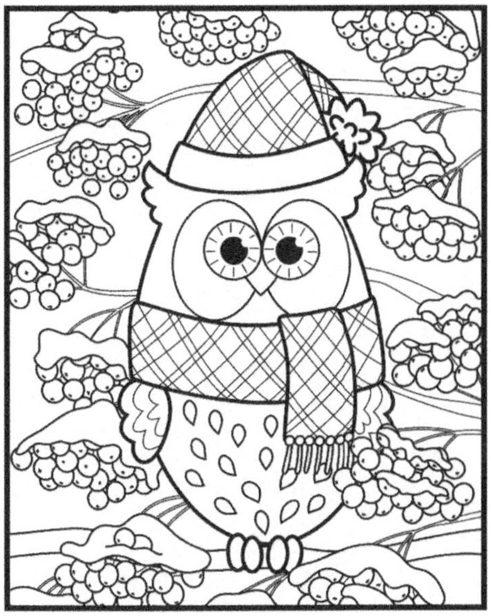
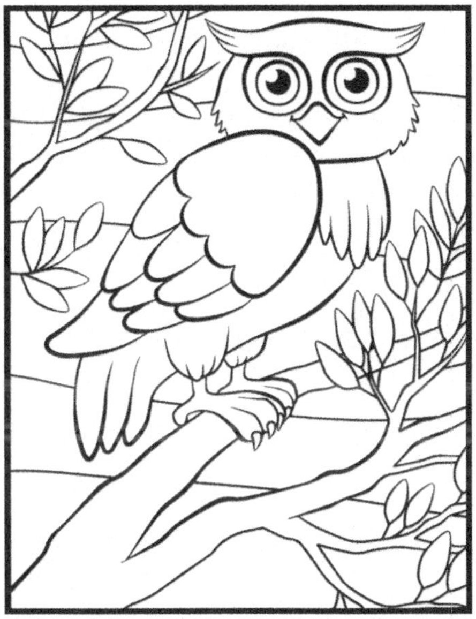
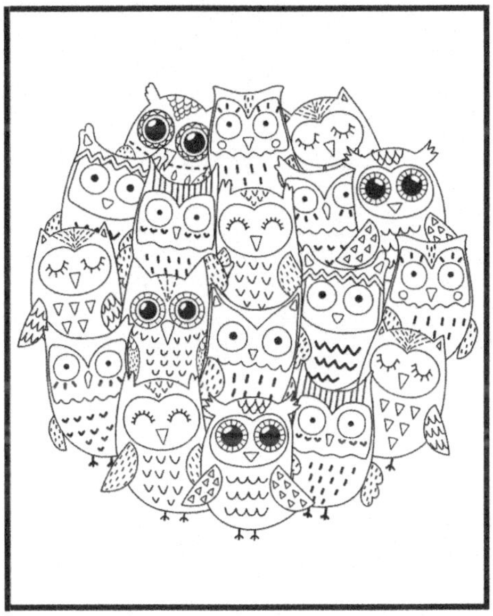
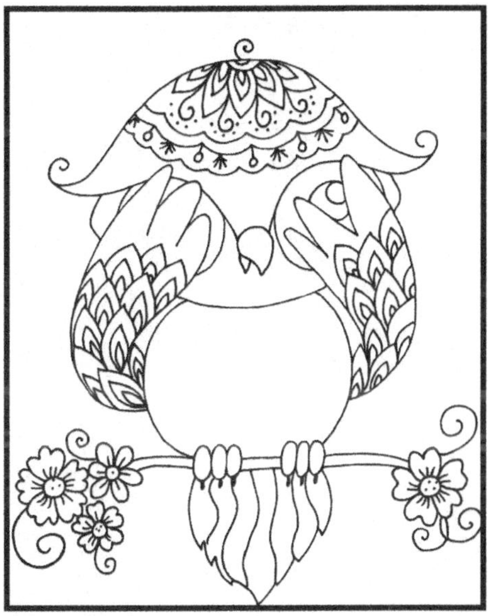
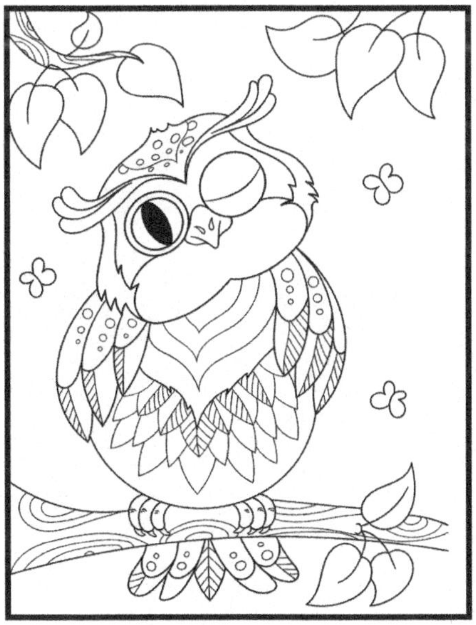
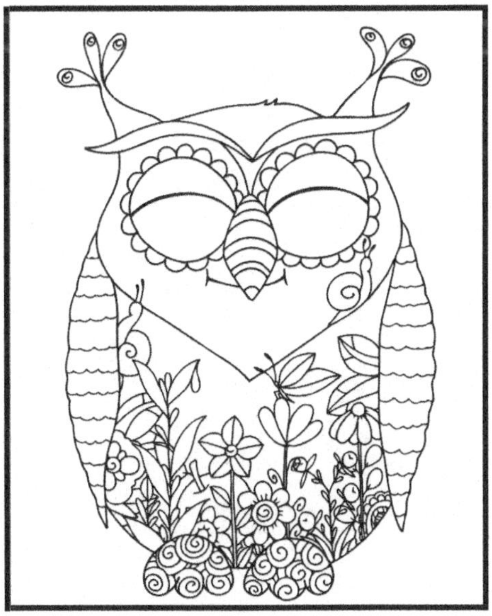
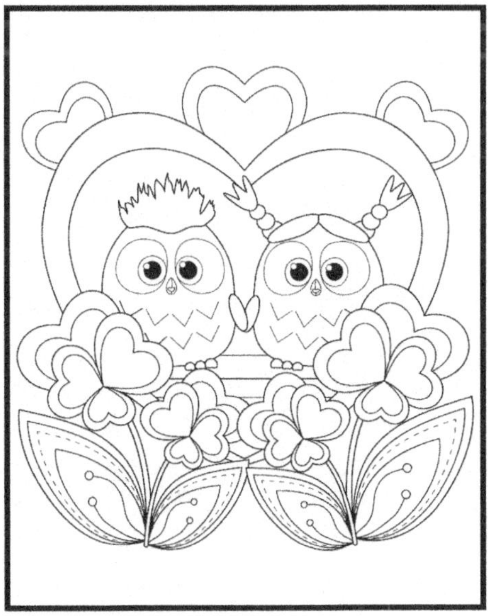

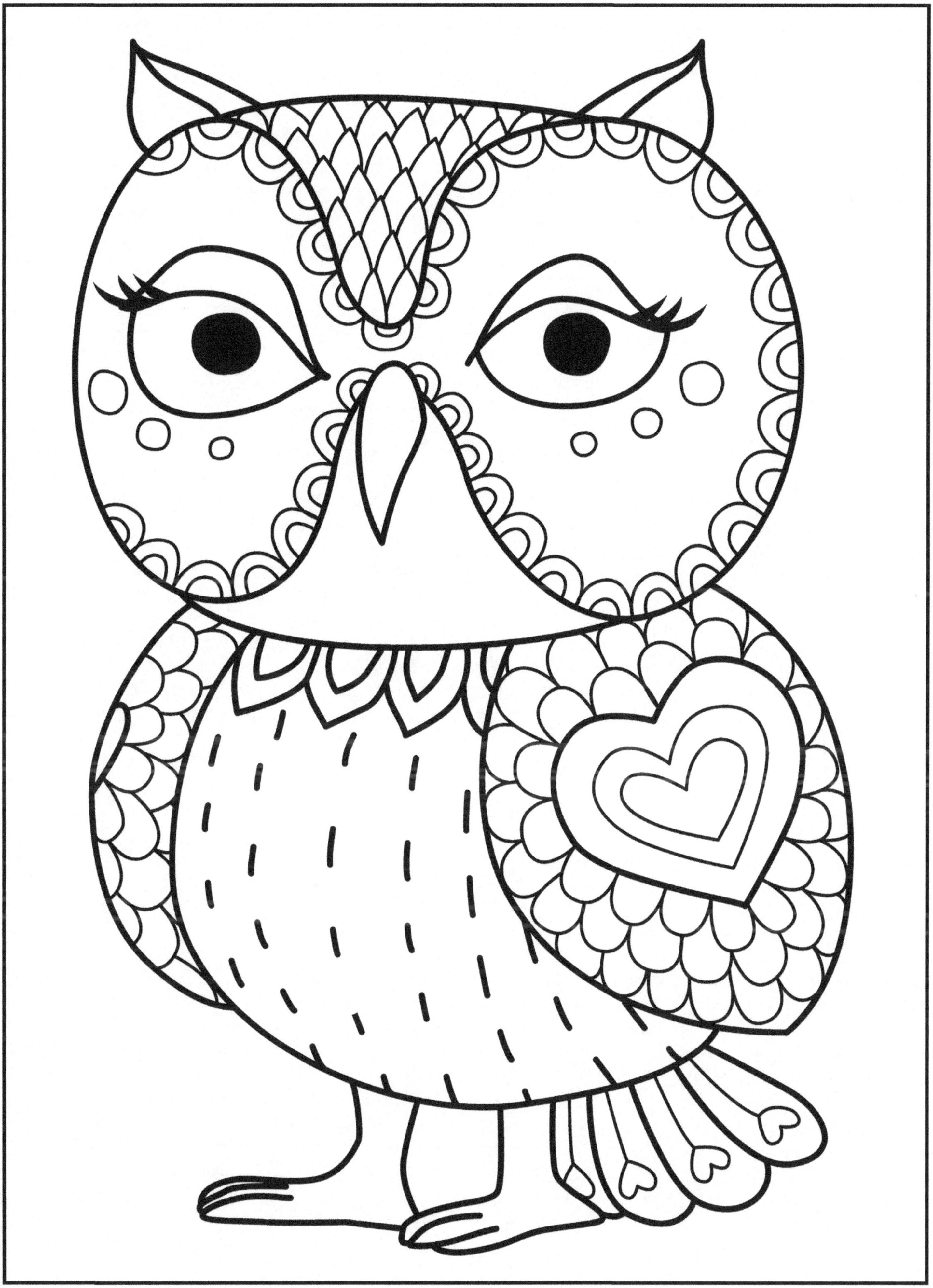

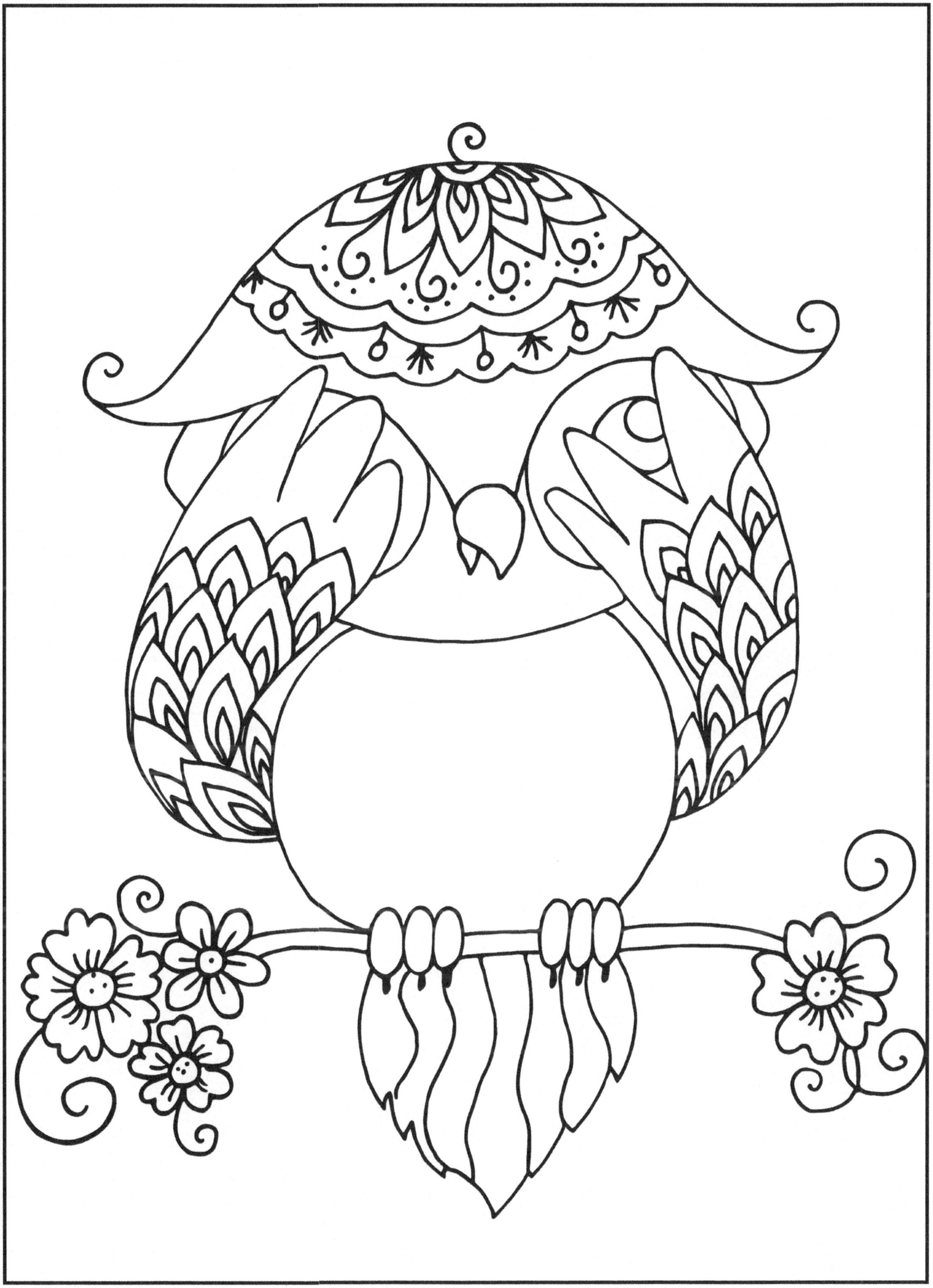

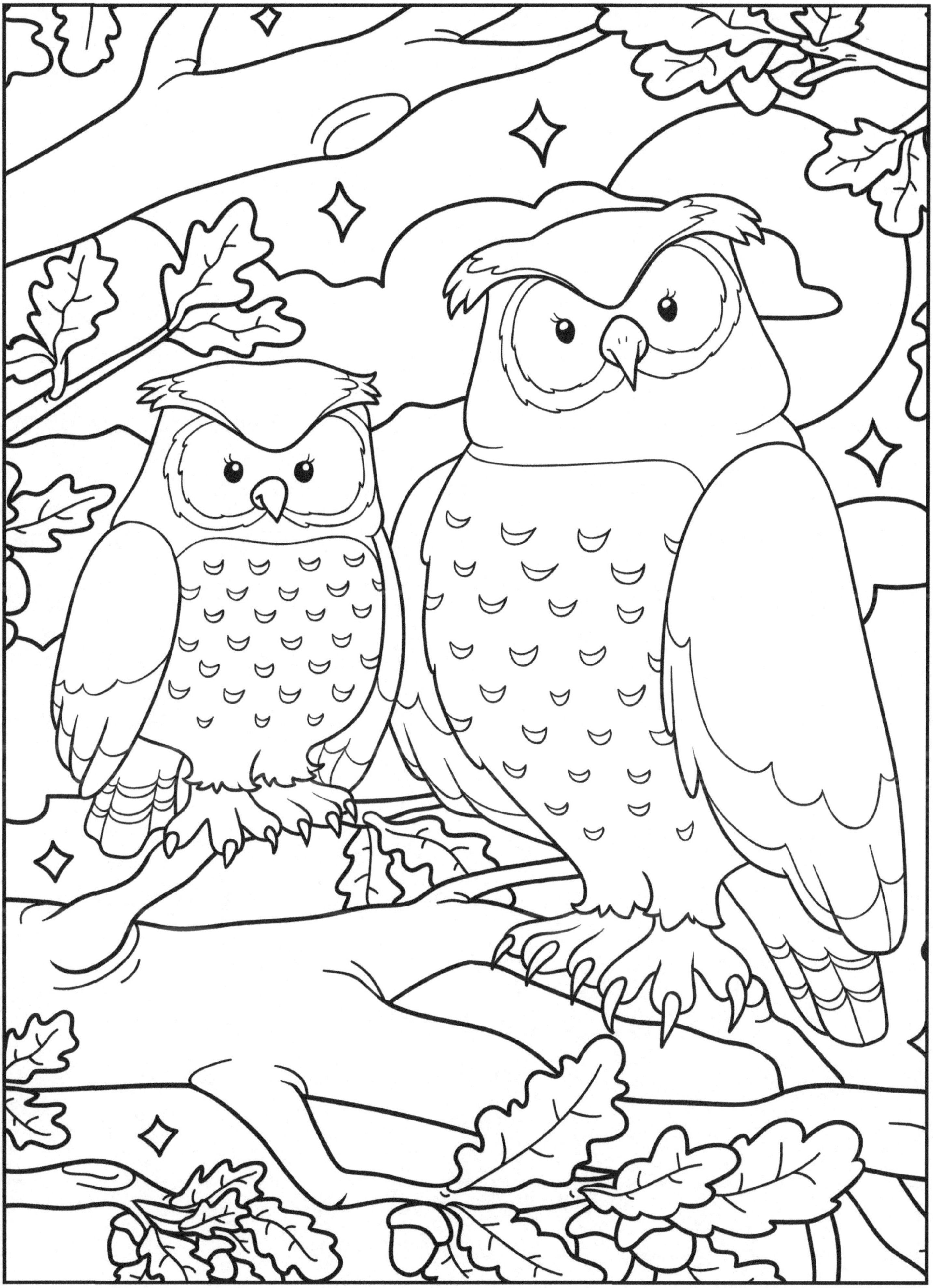

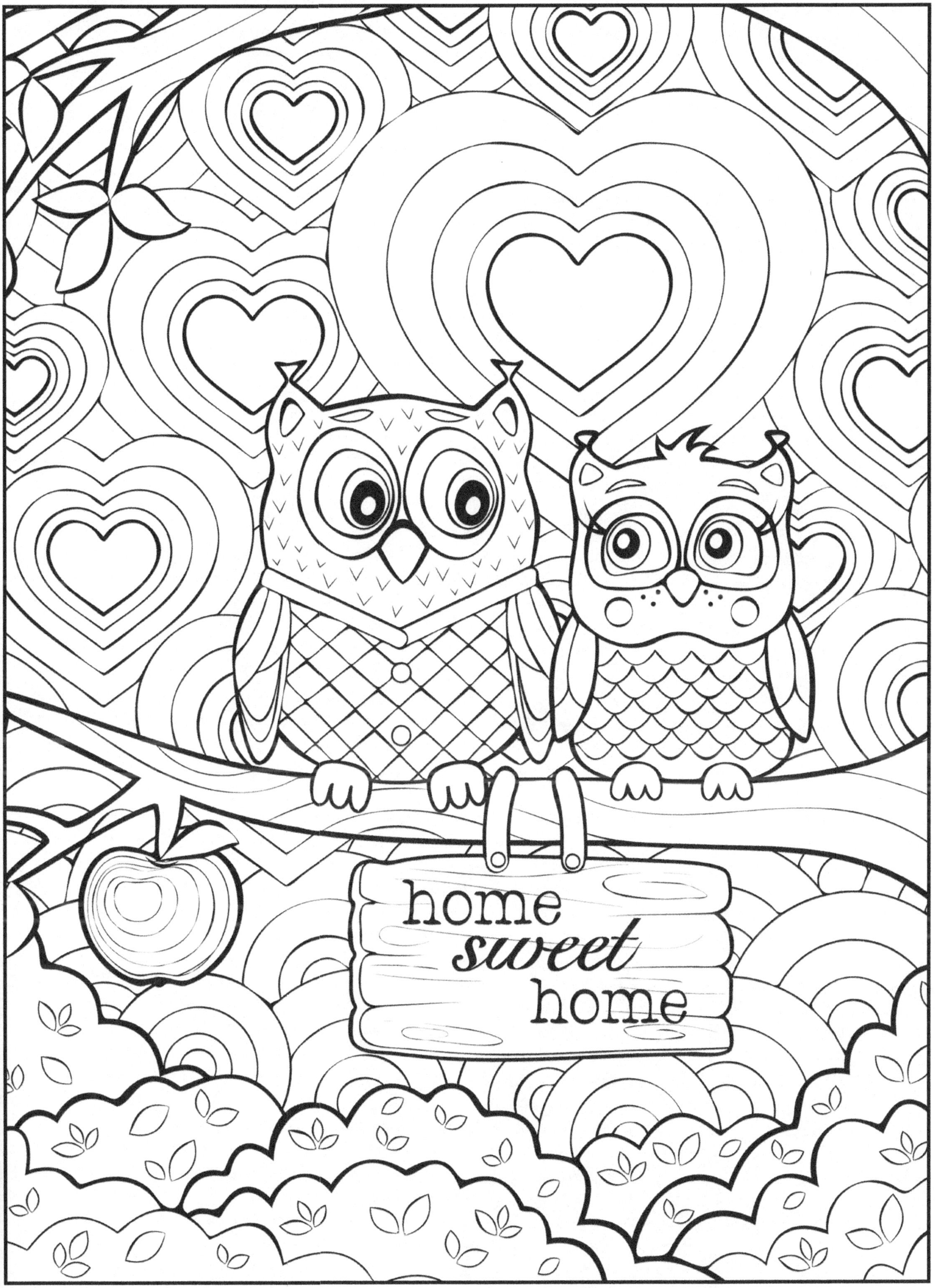
home
sweet
home

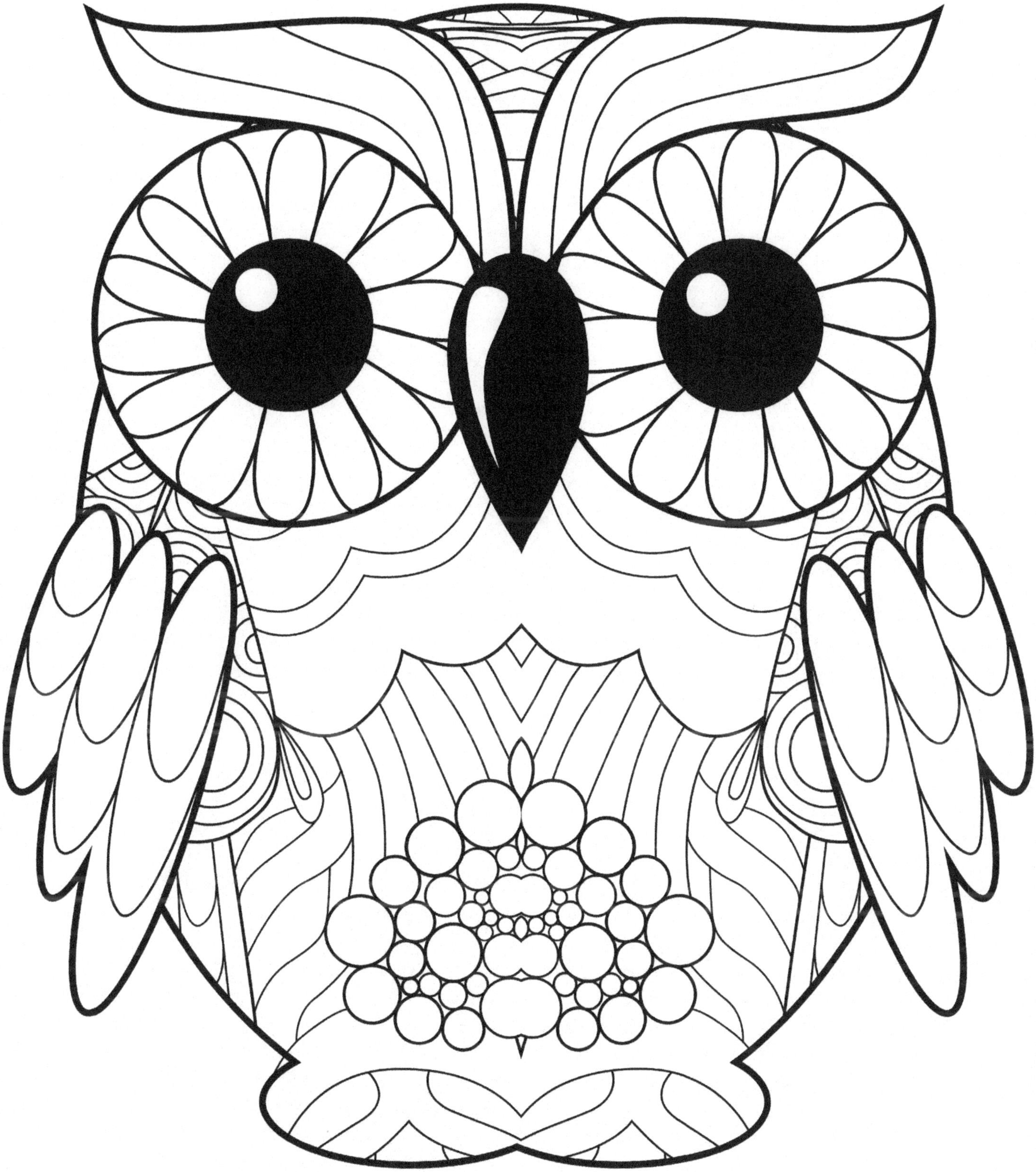

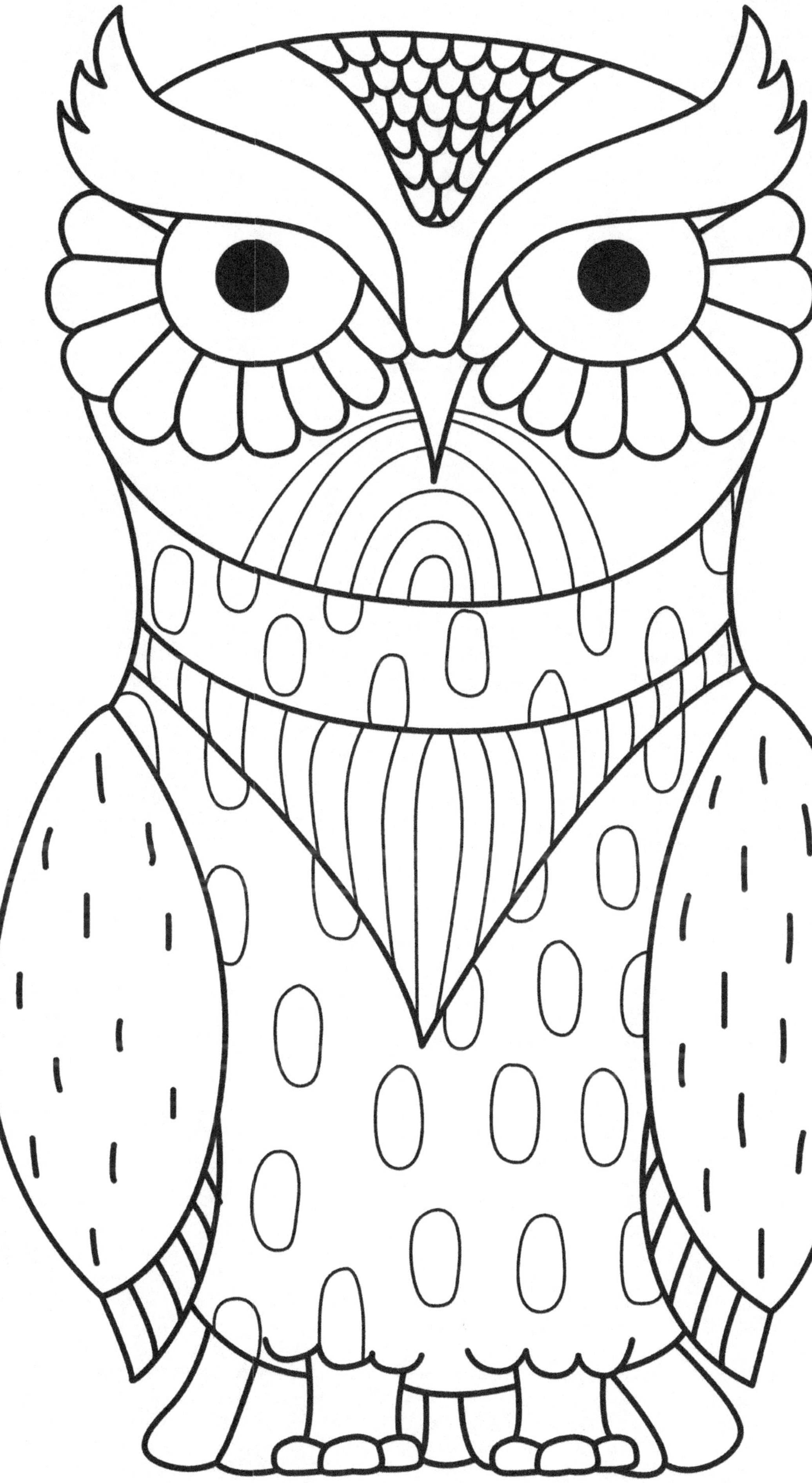

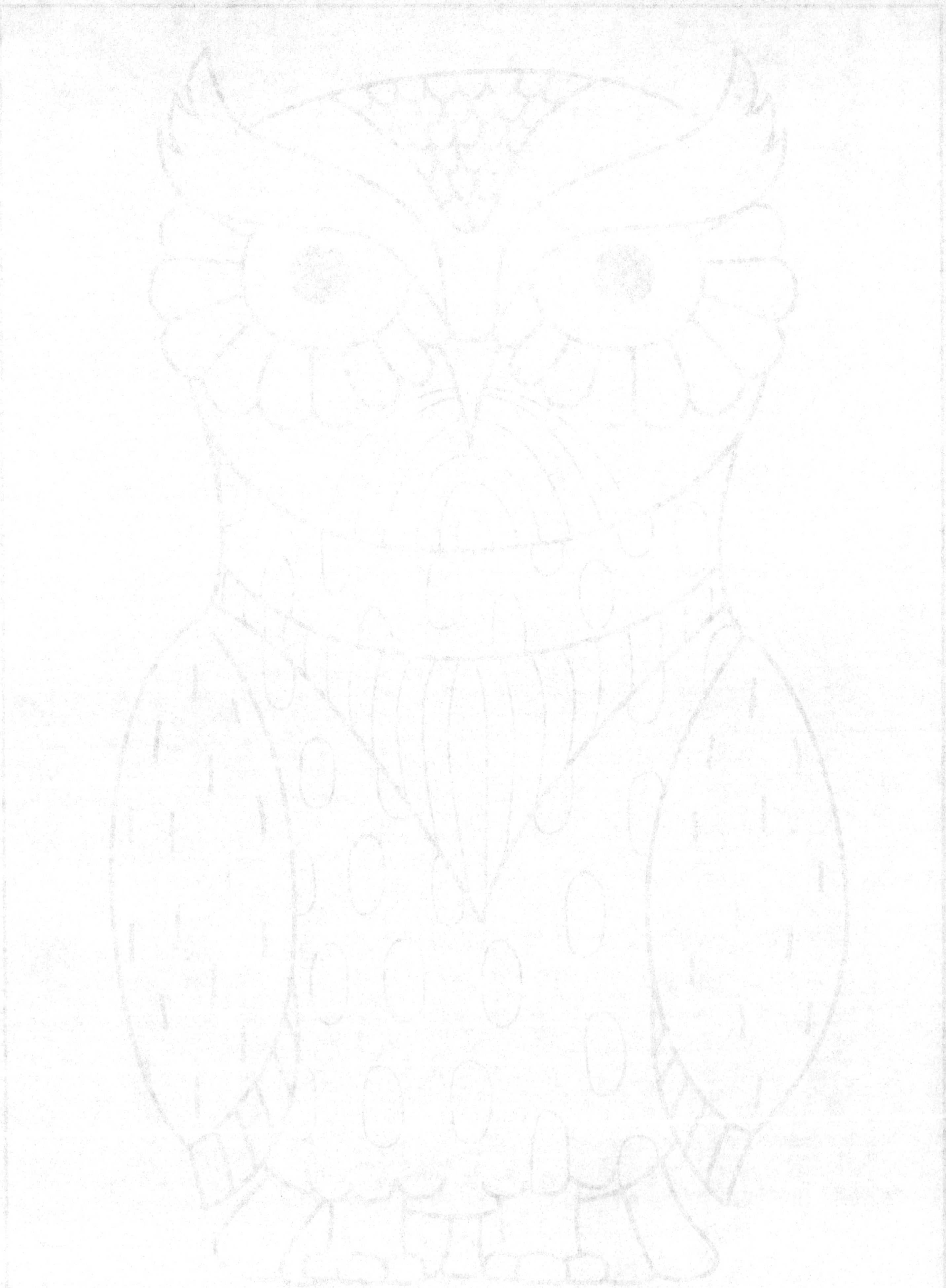

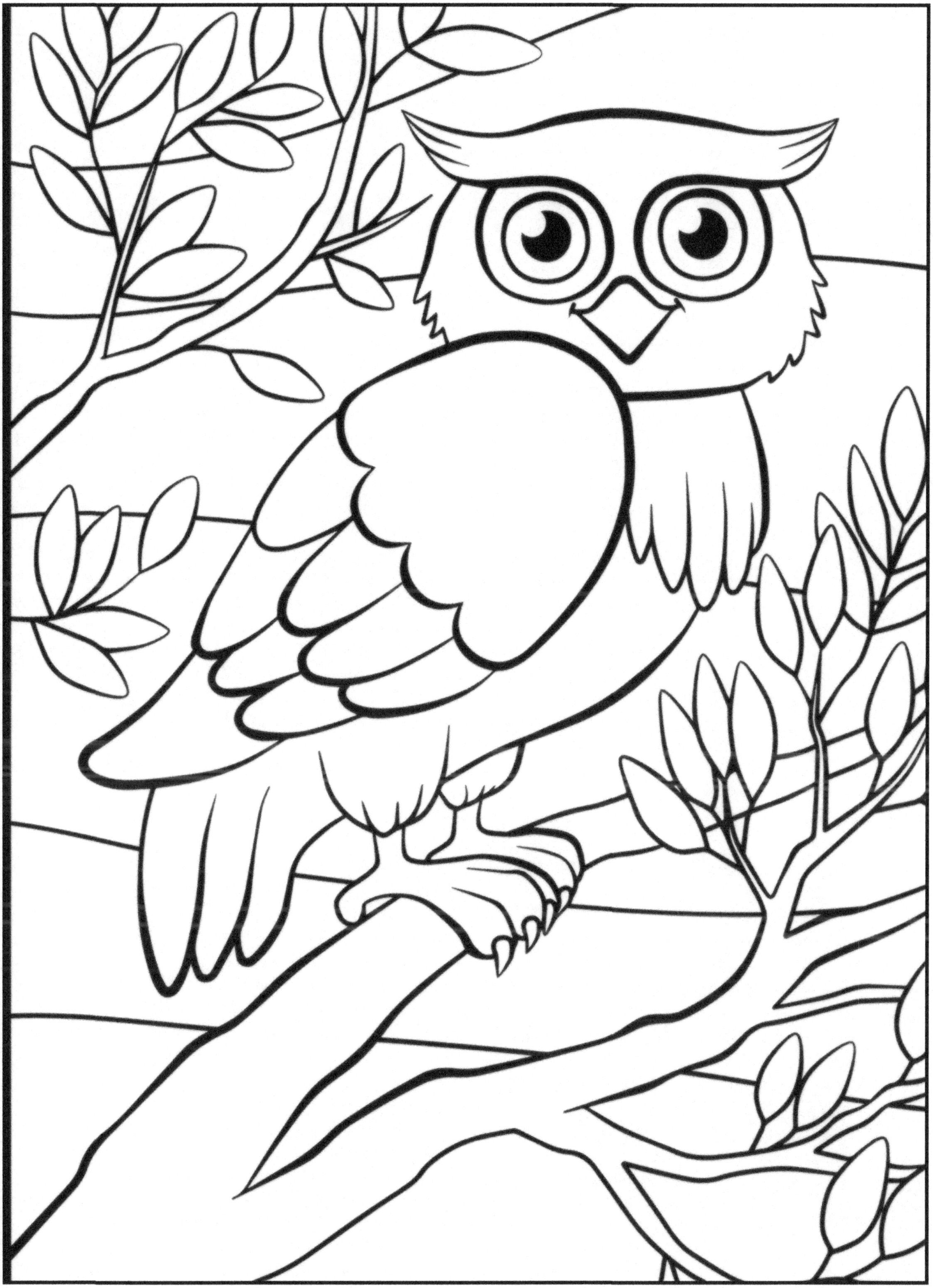

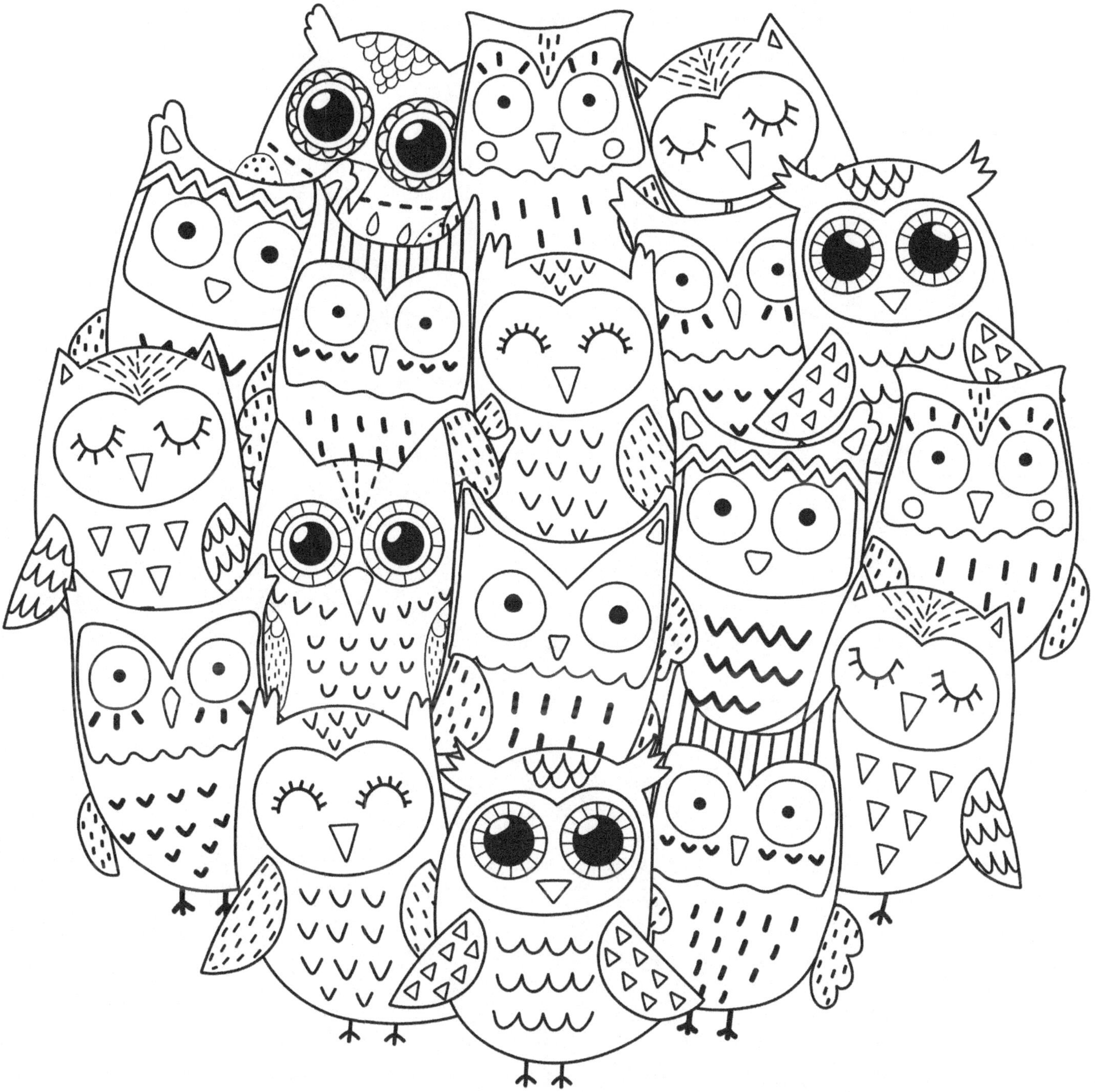

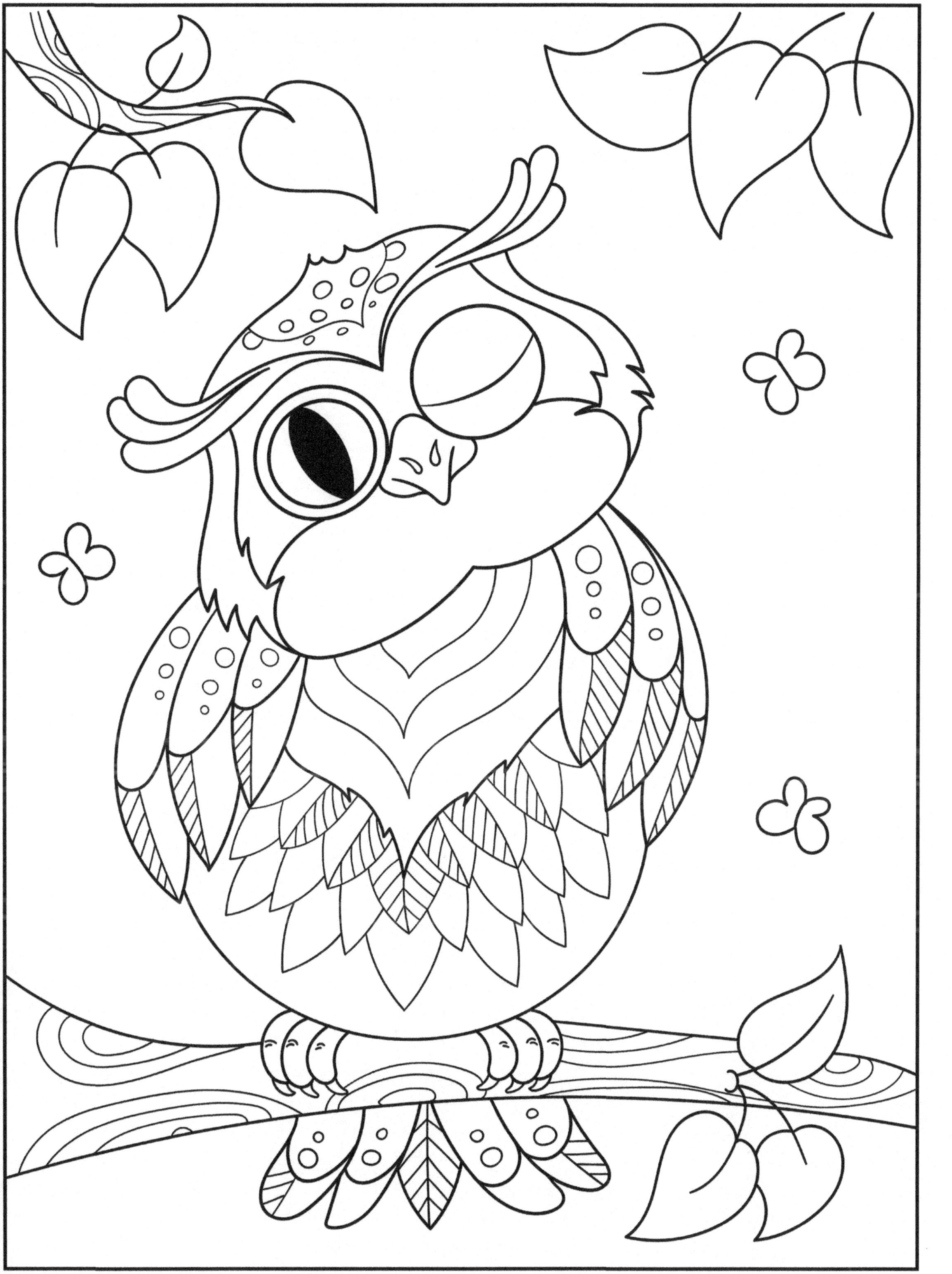

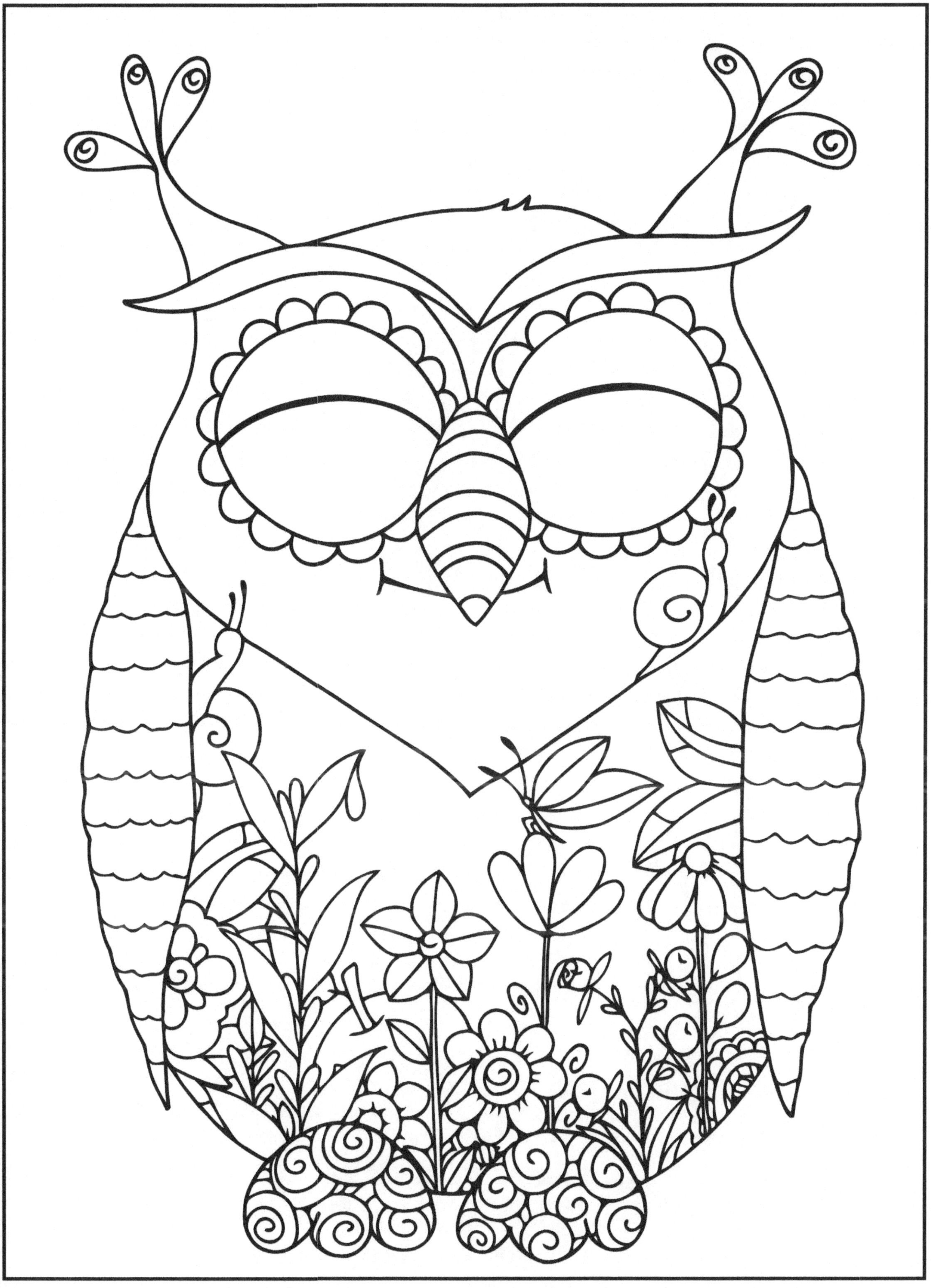

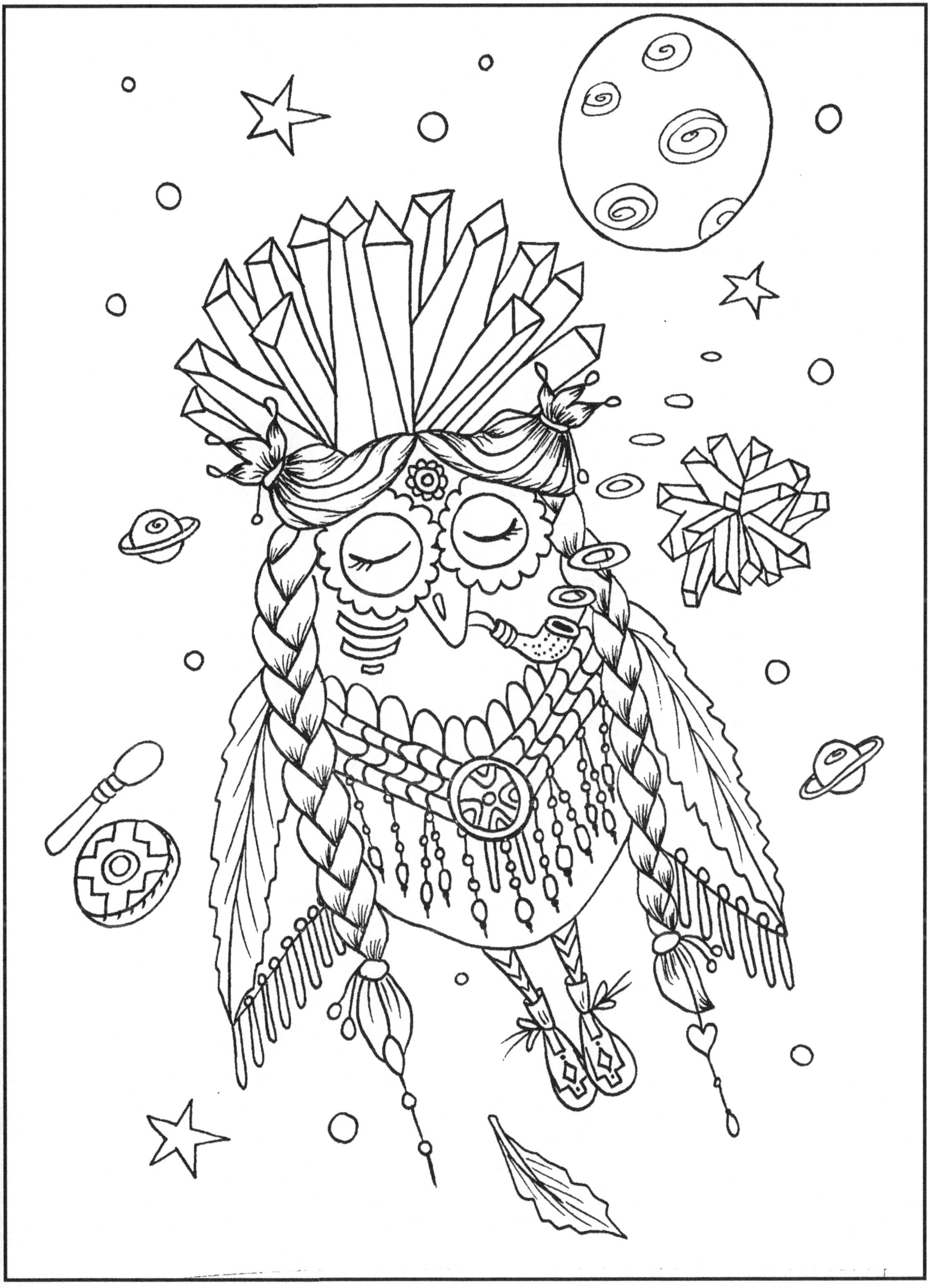

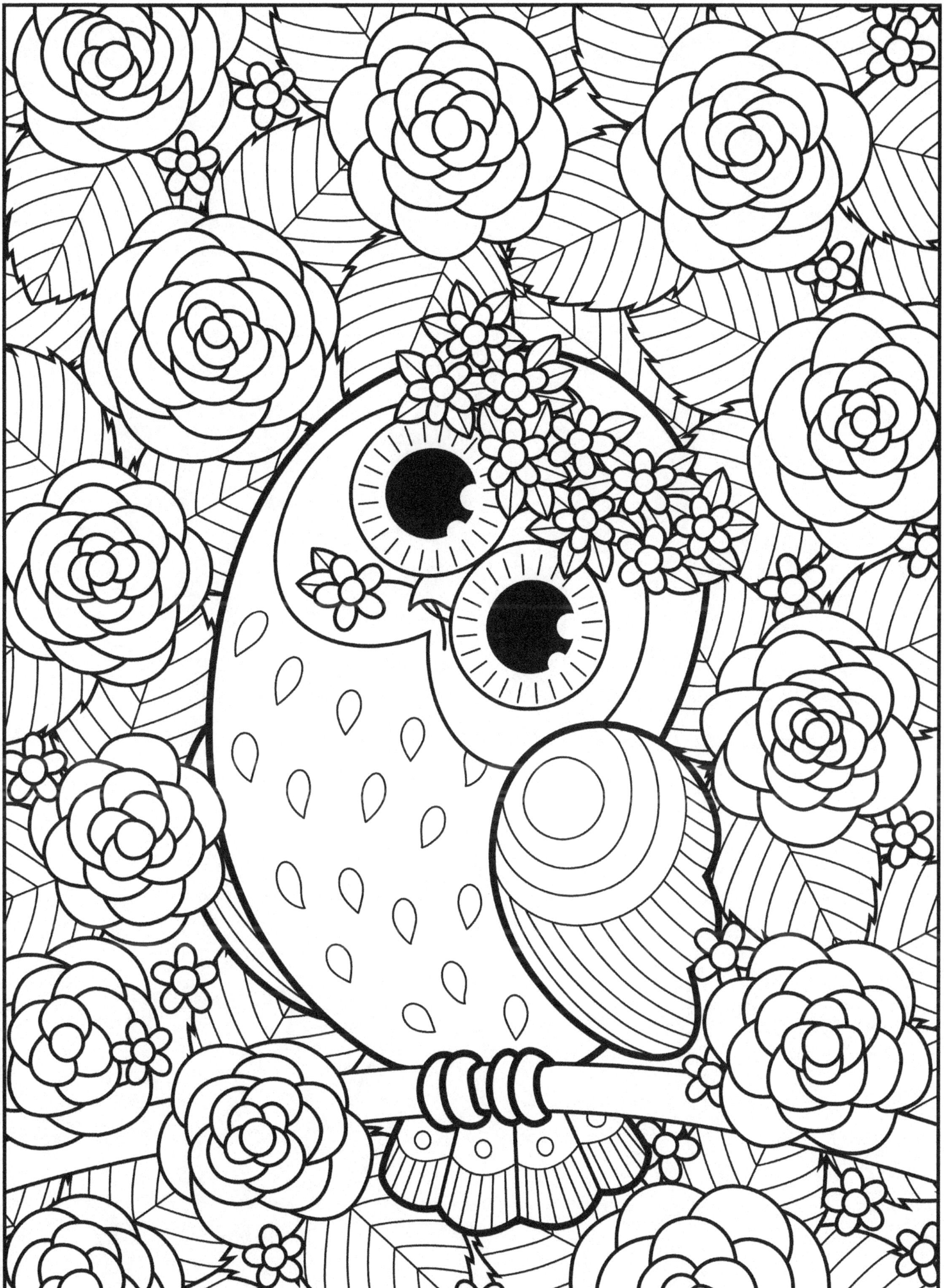

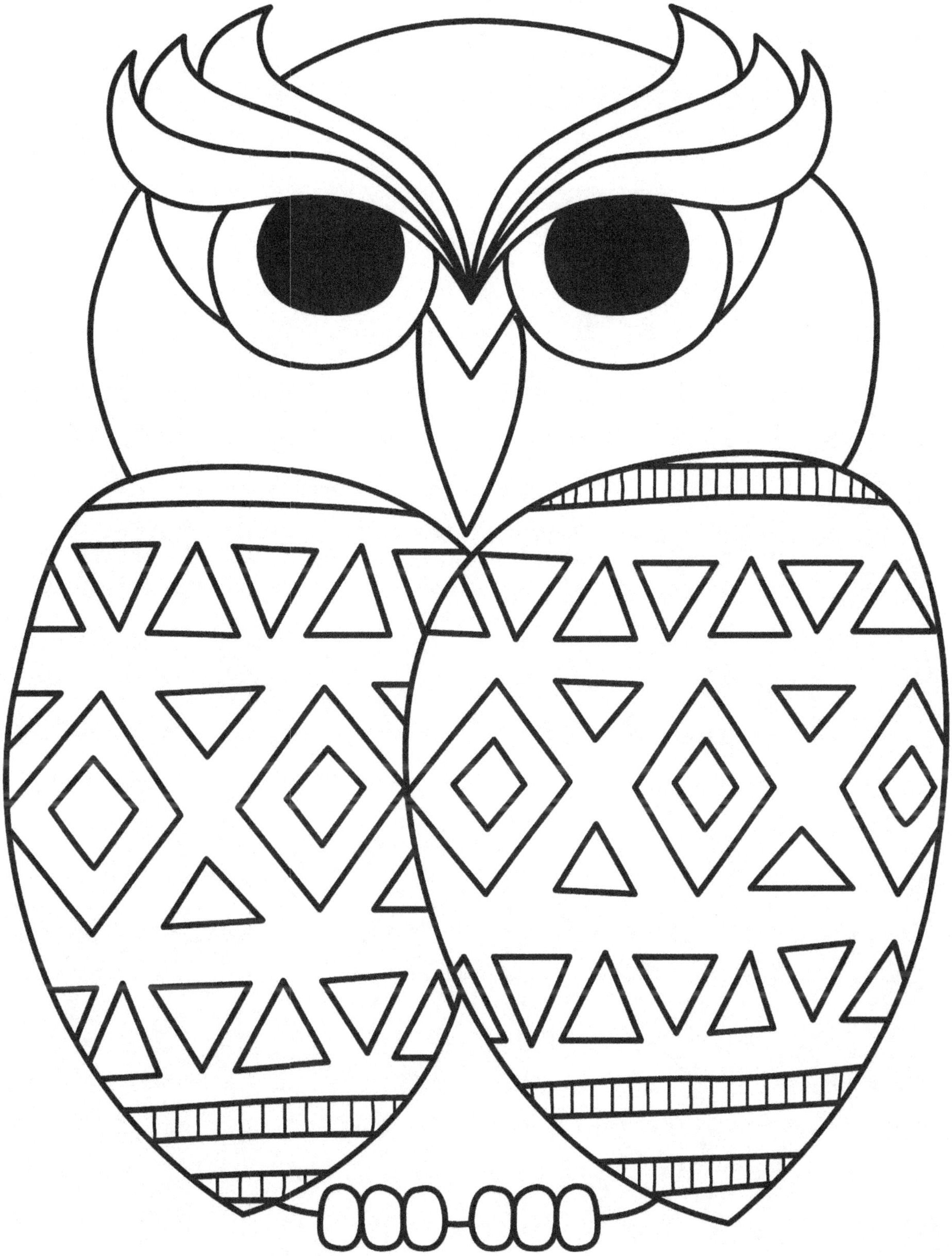

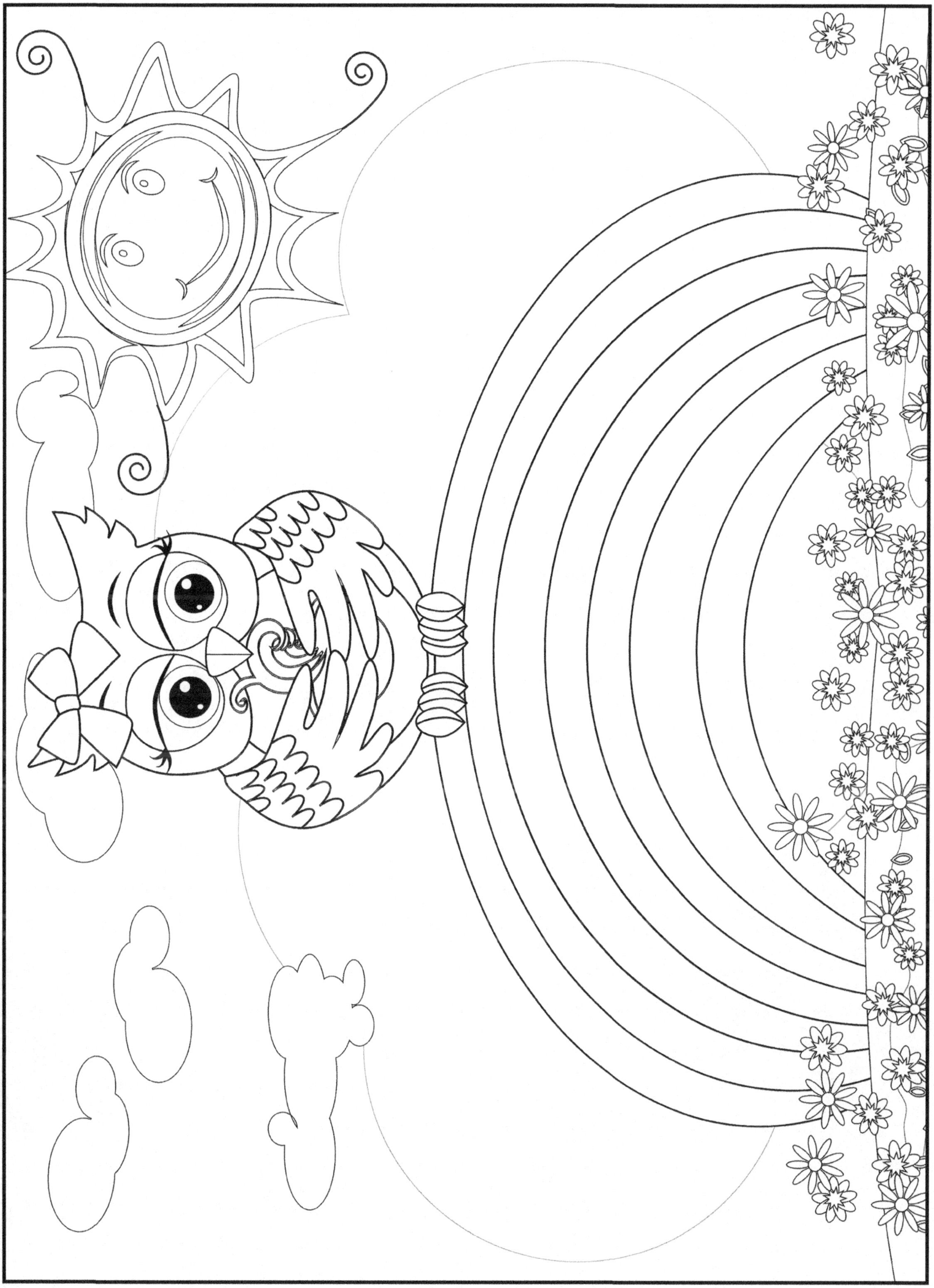

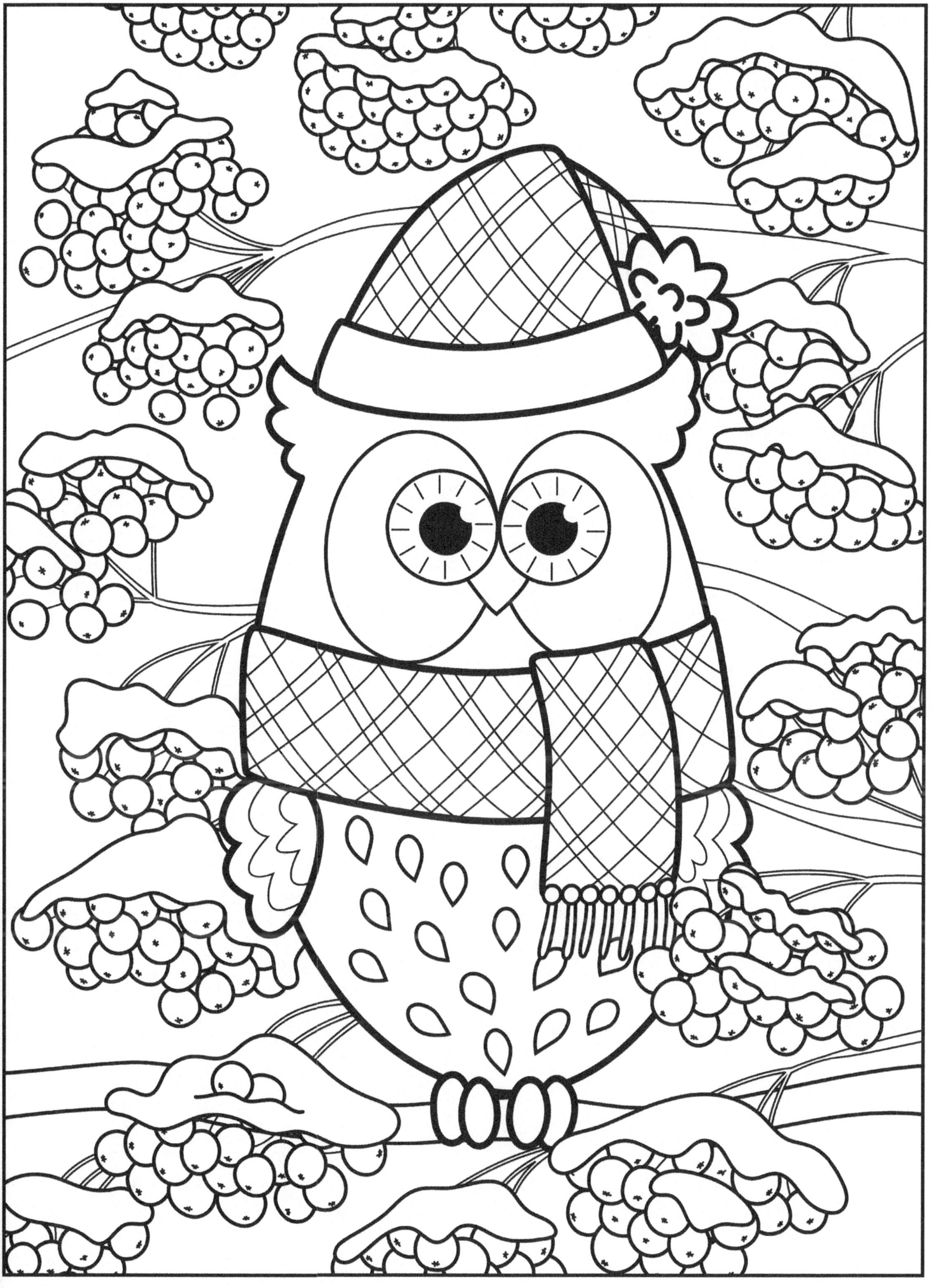

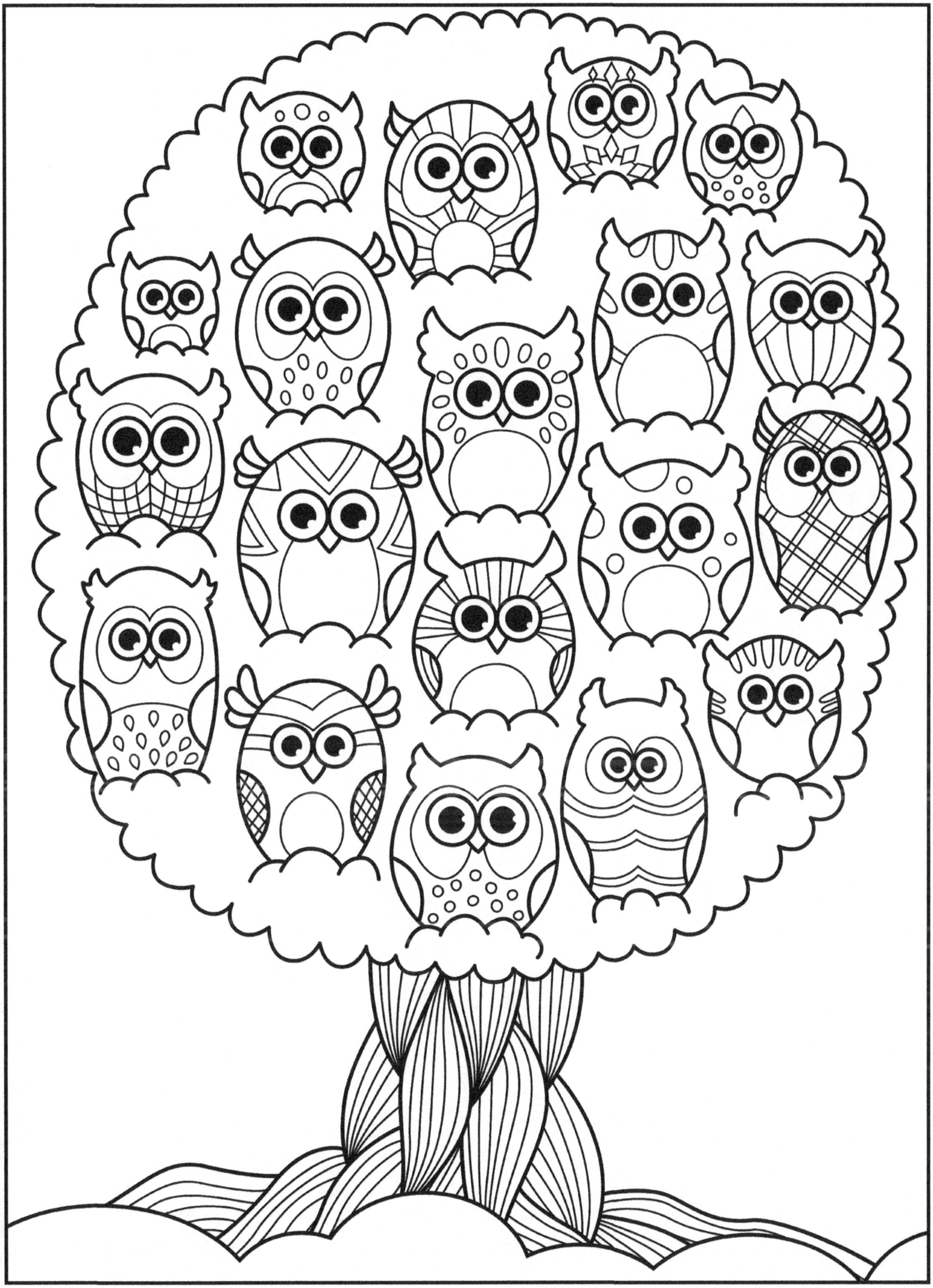

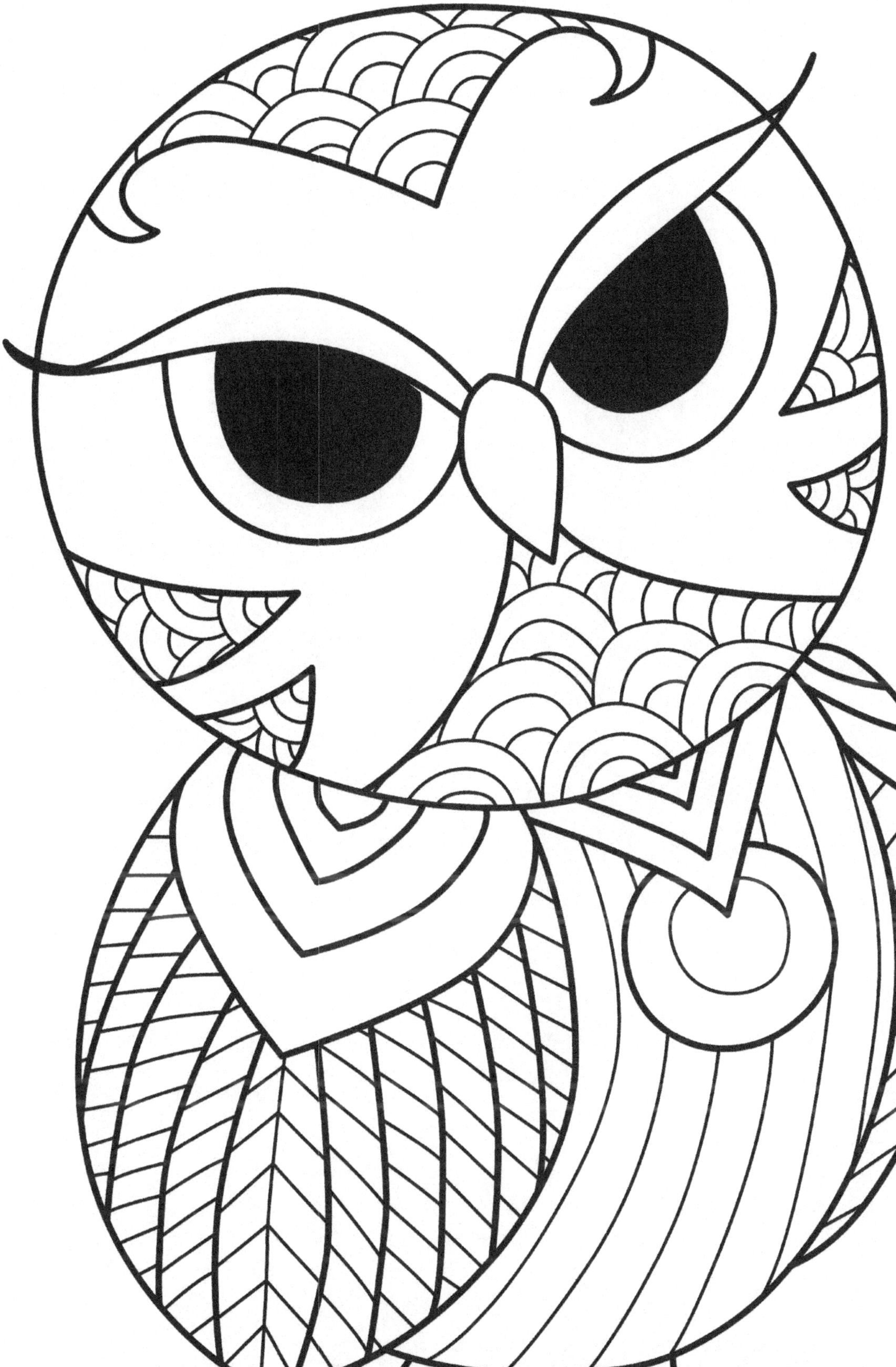

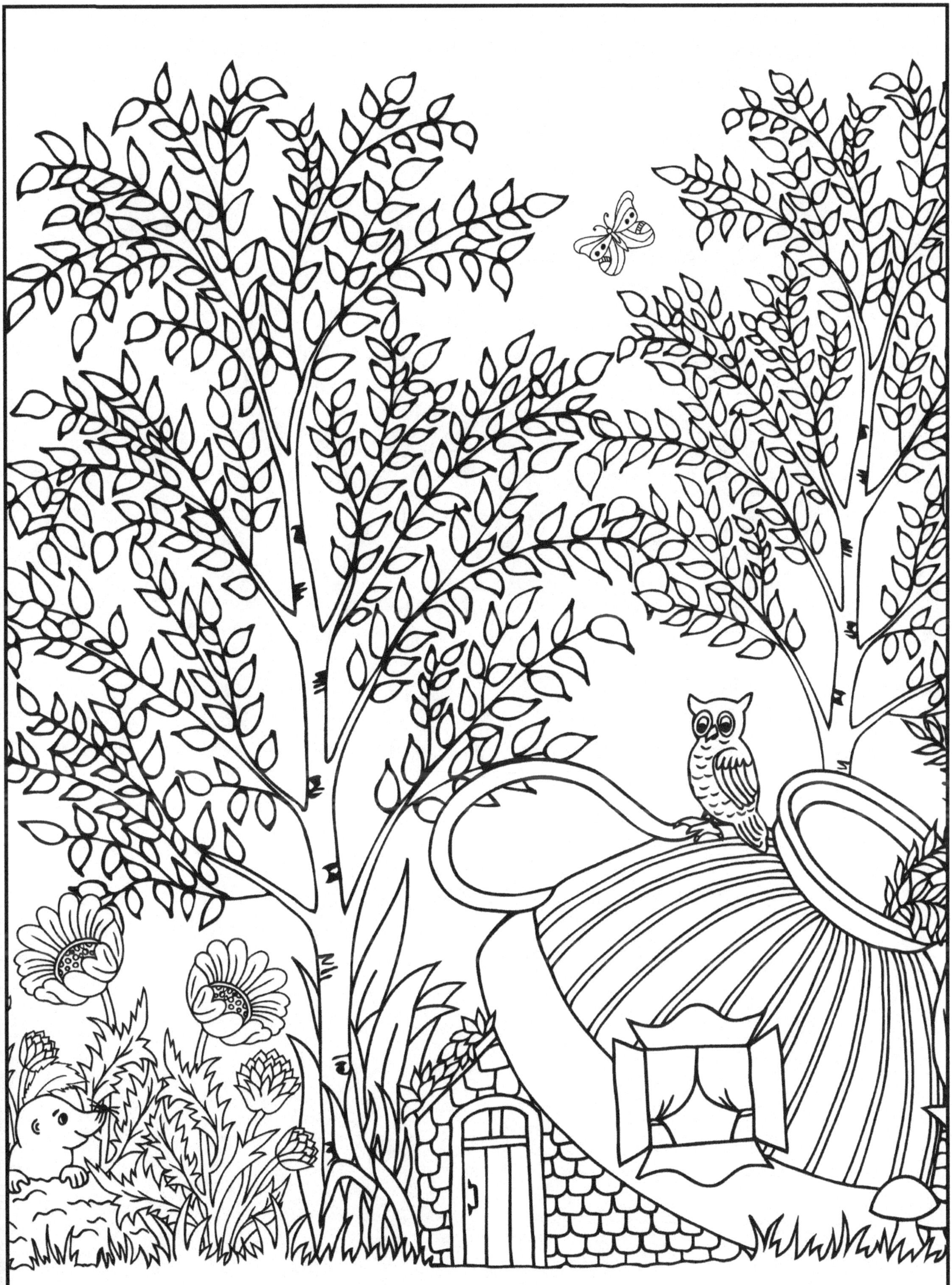

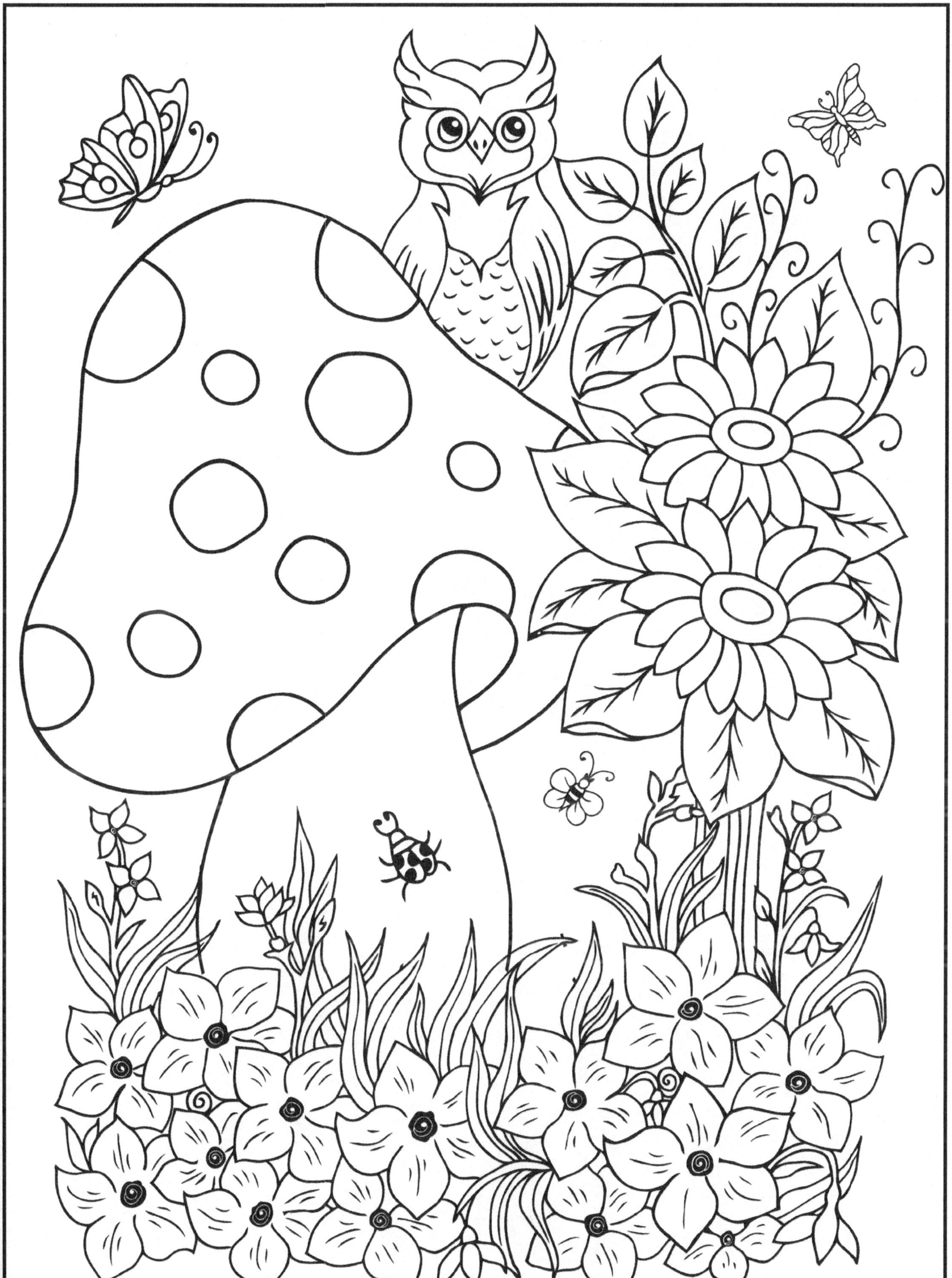

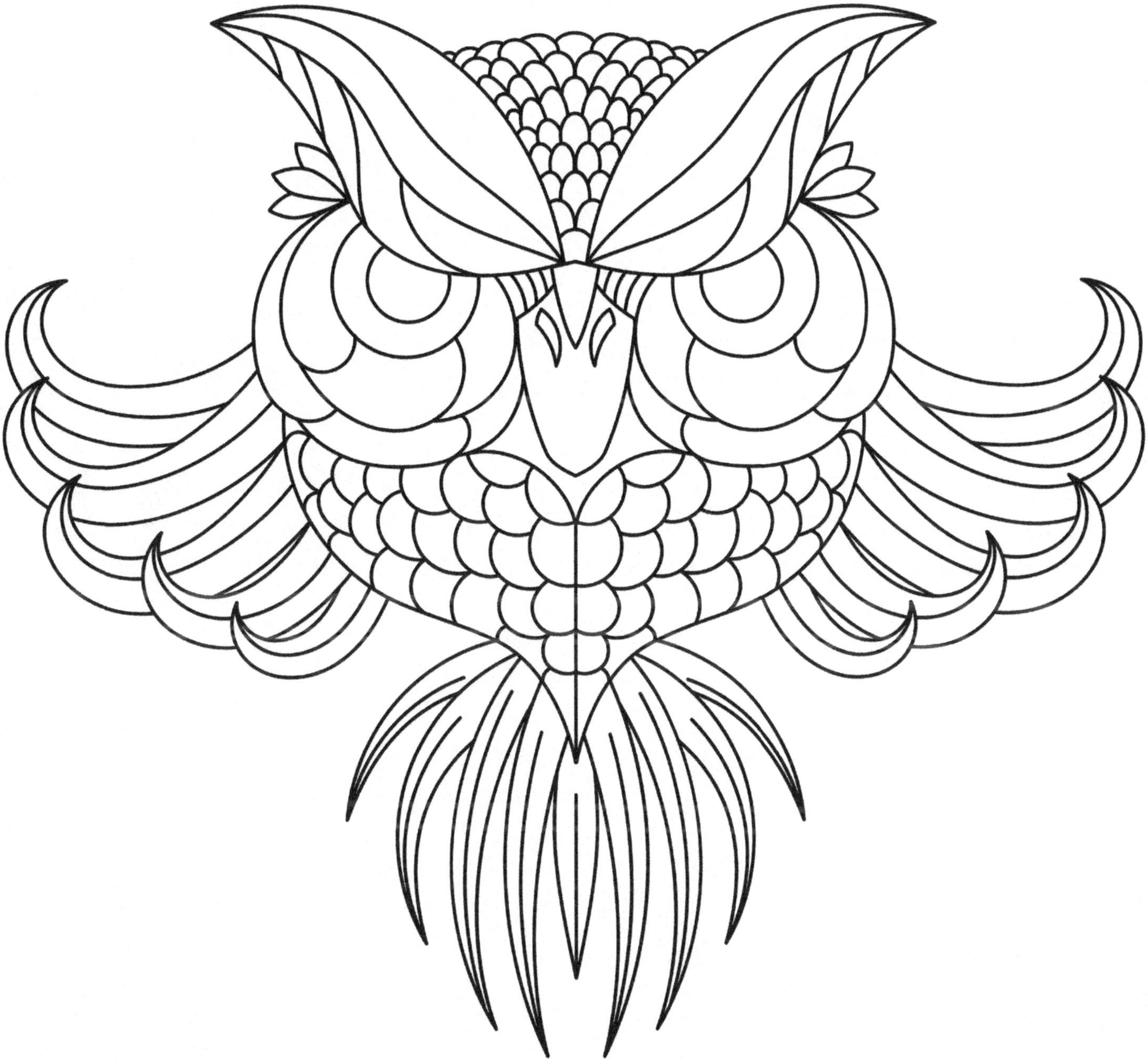

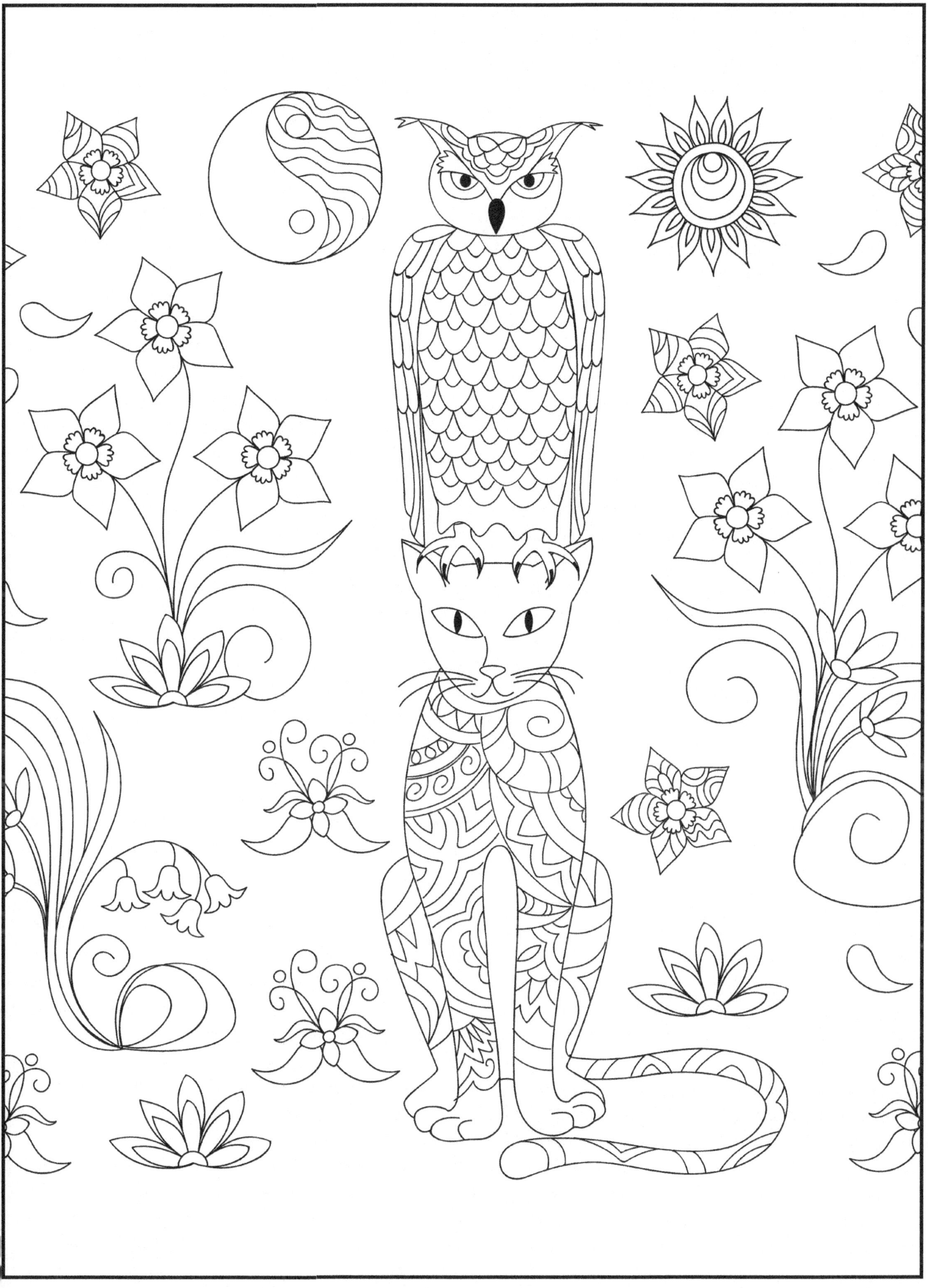

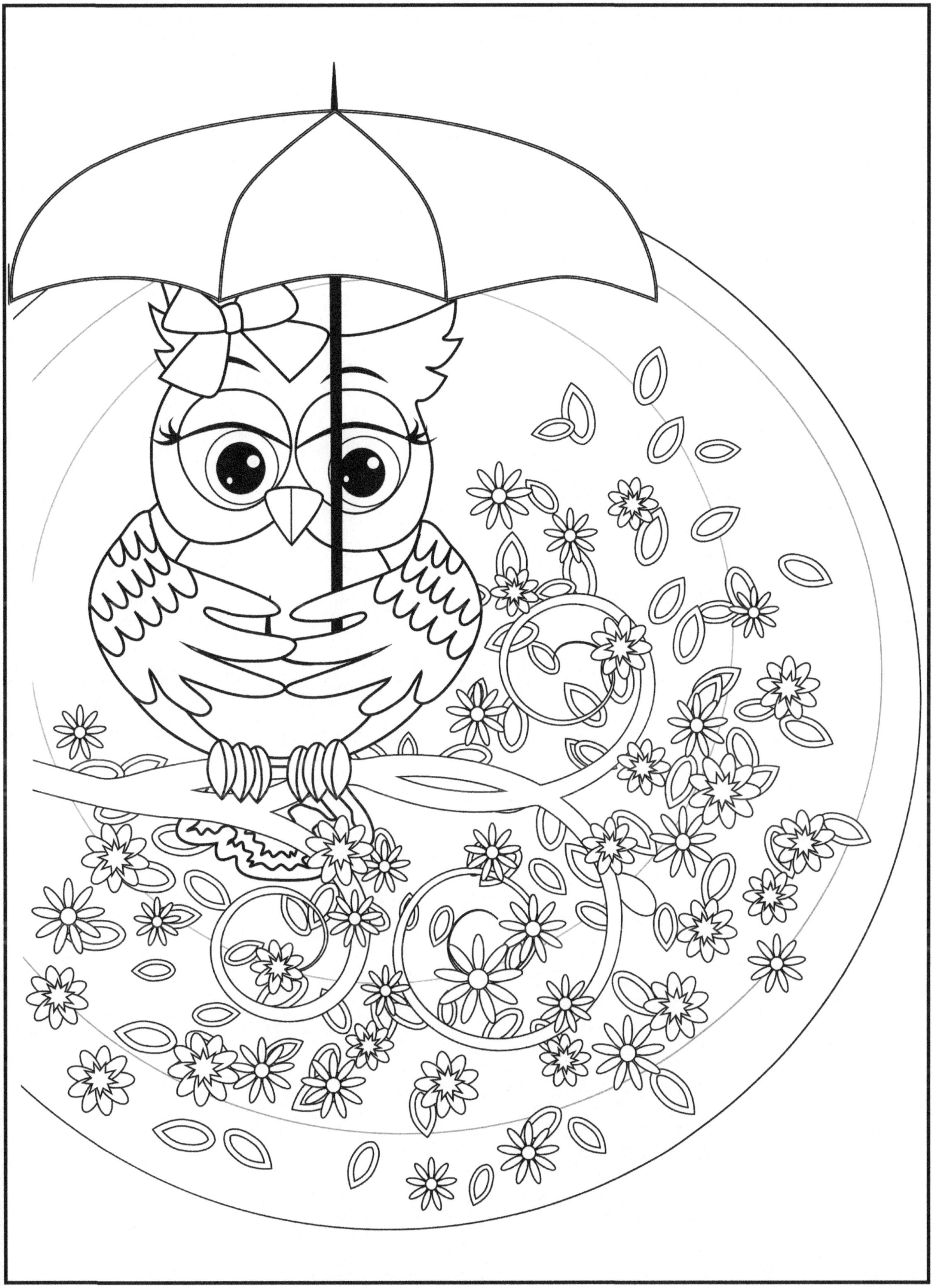

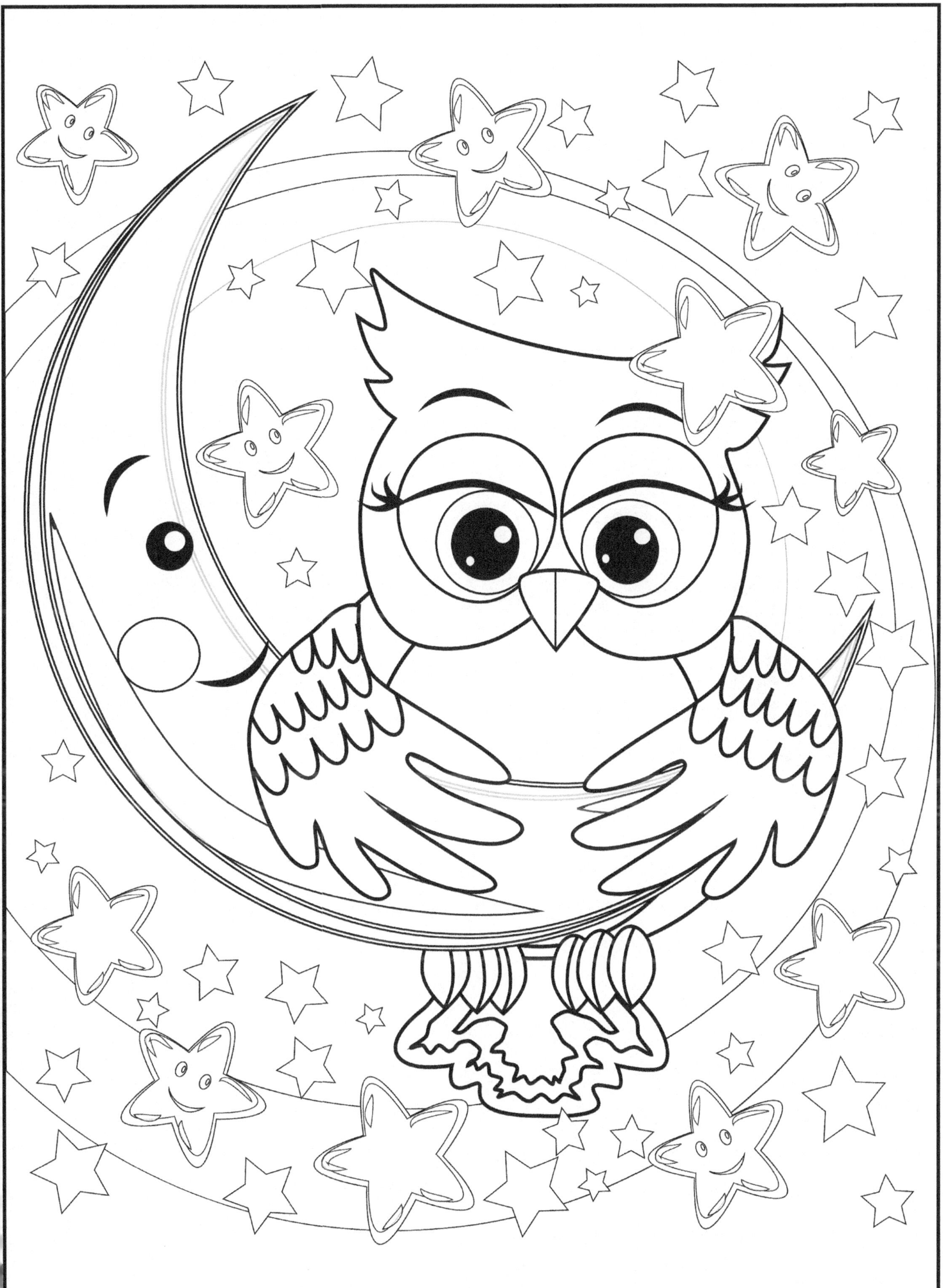

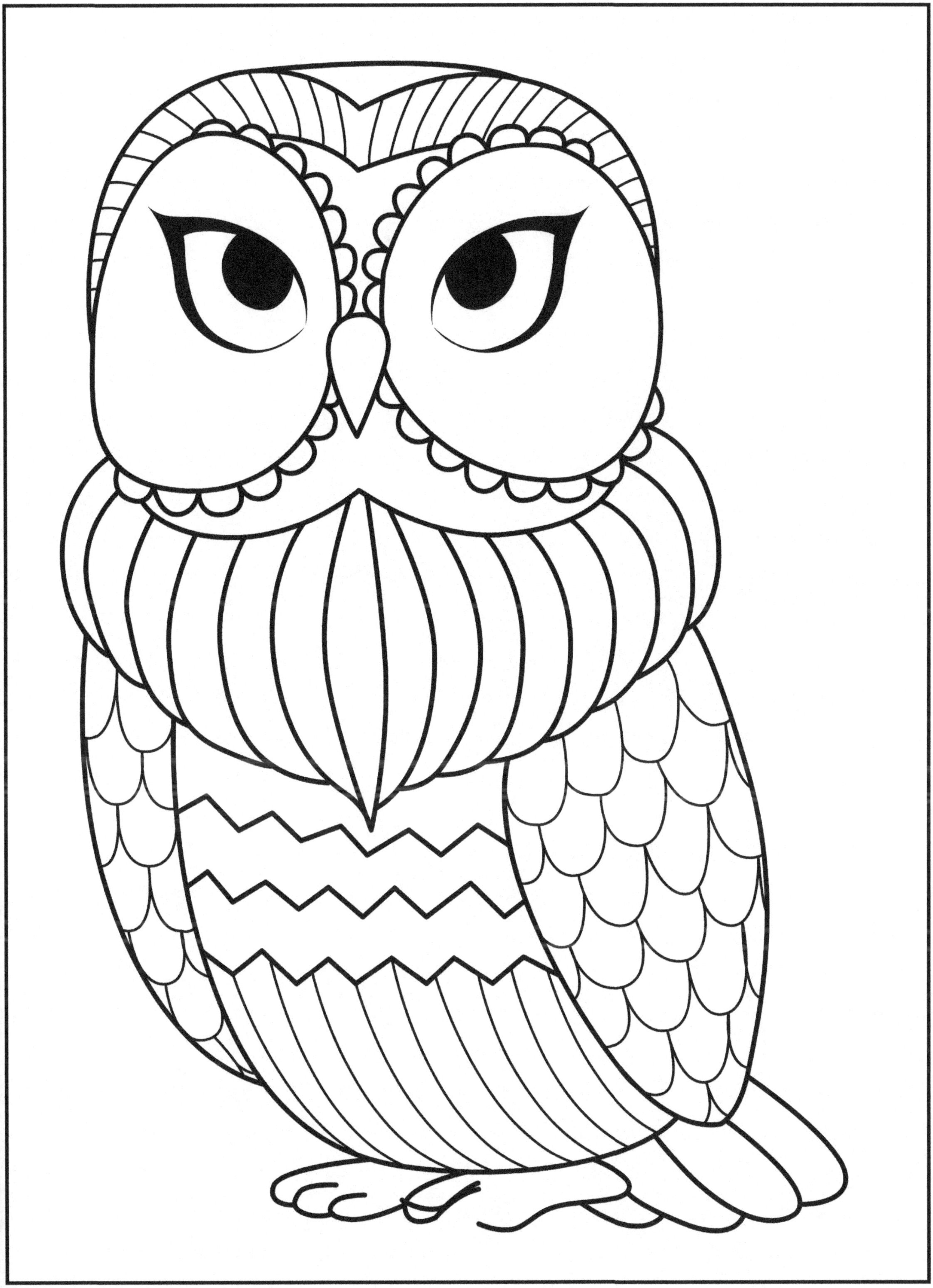

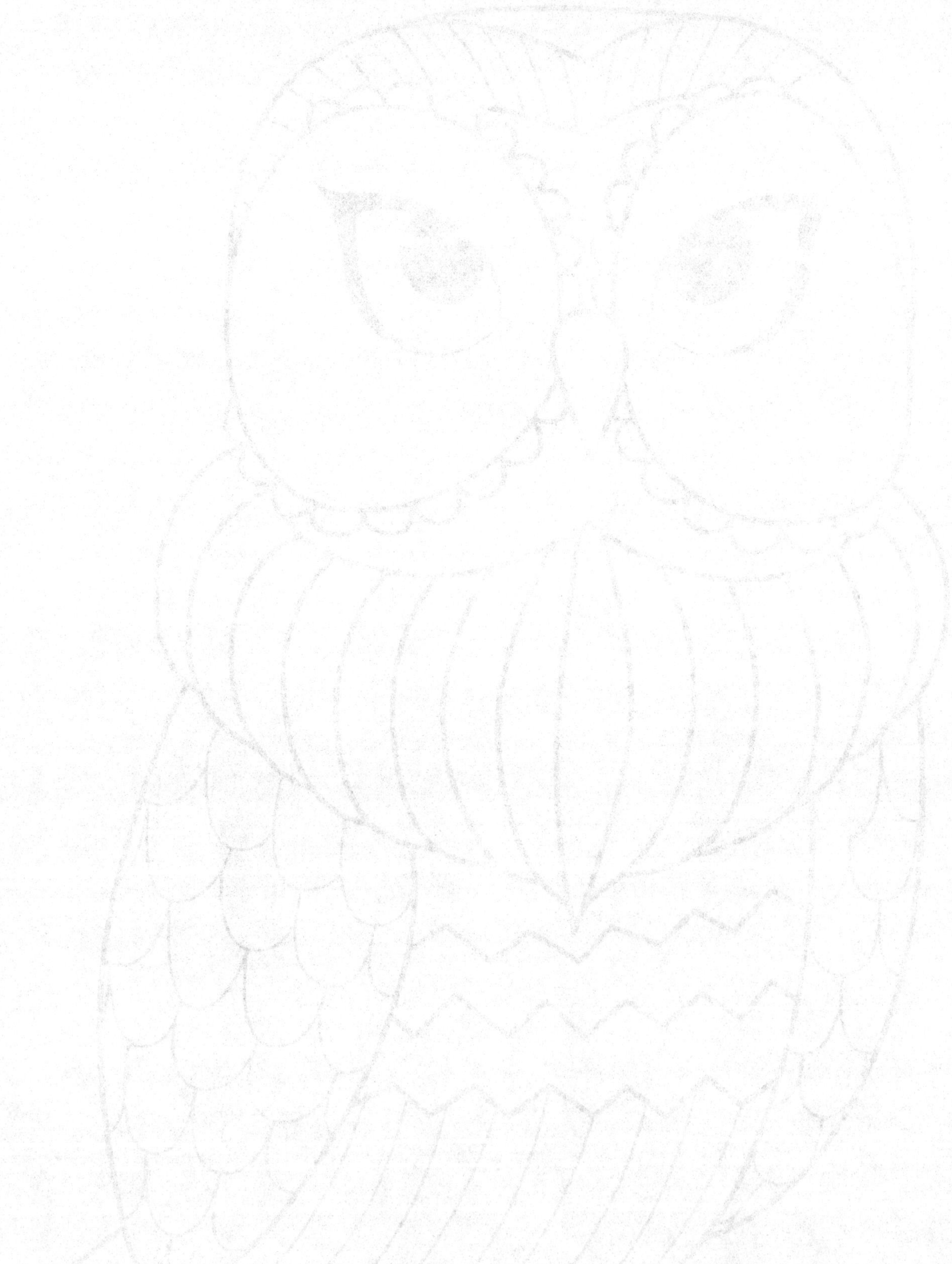

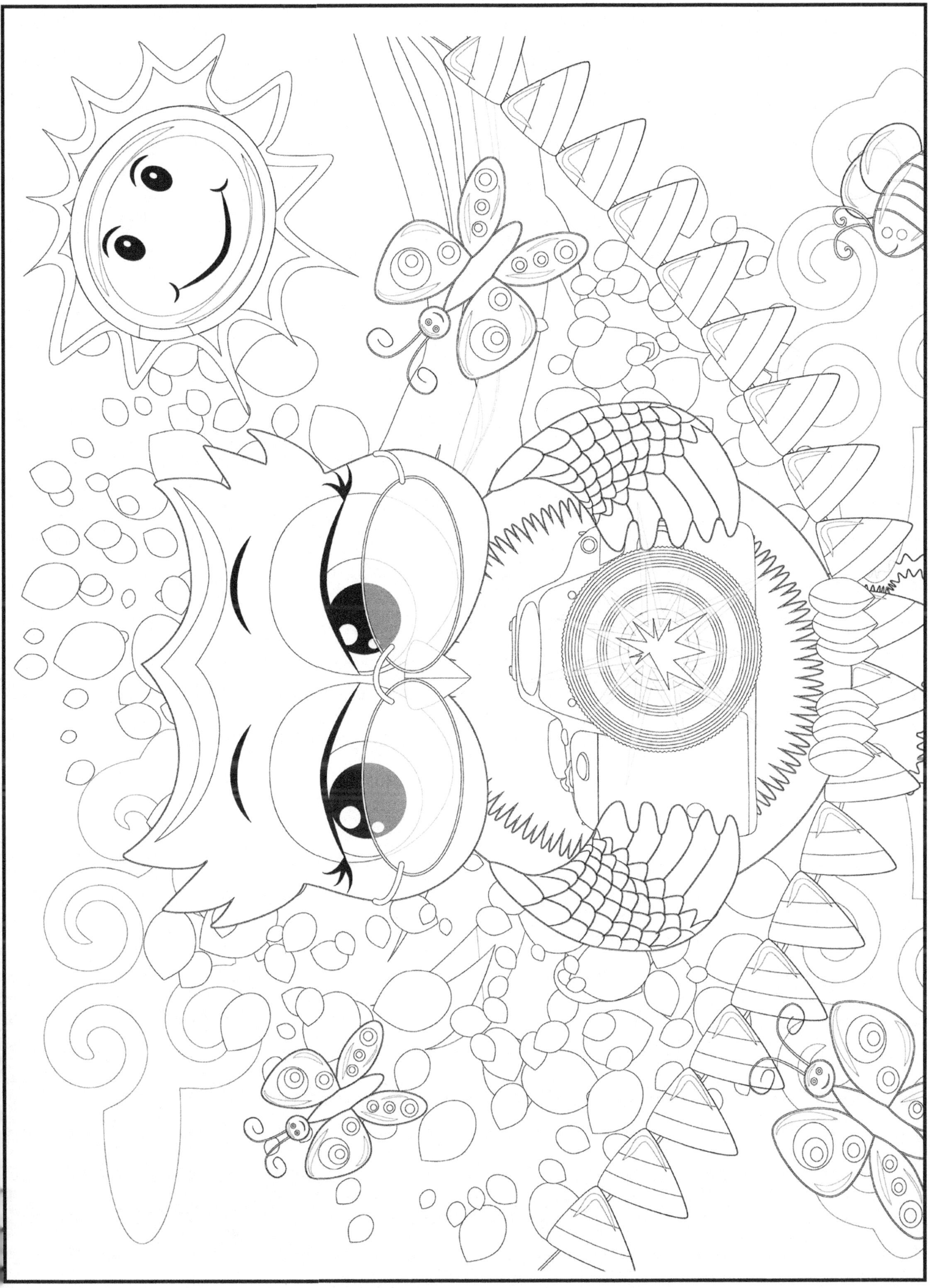

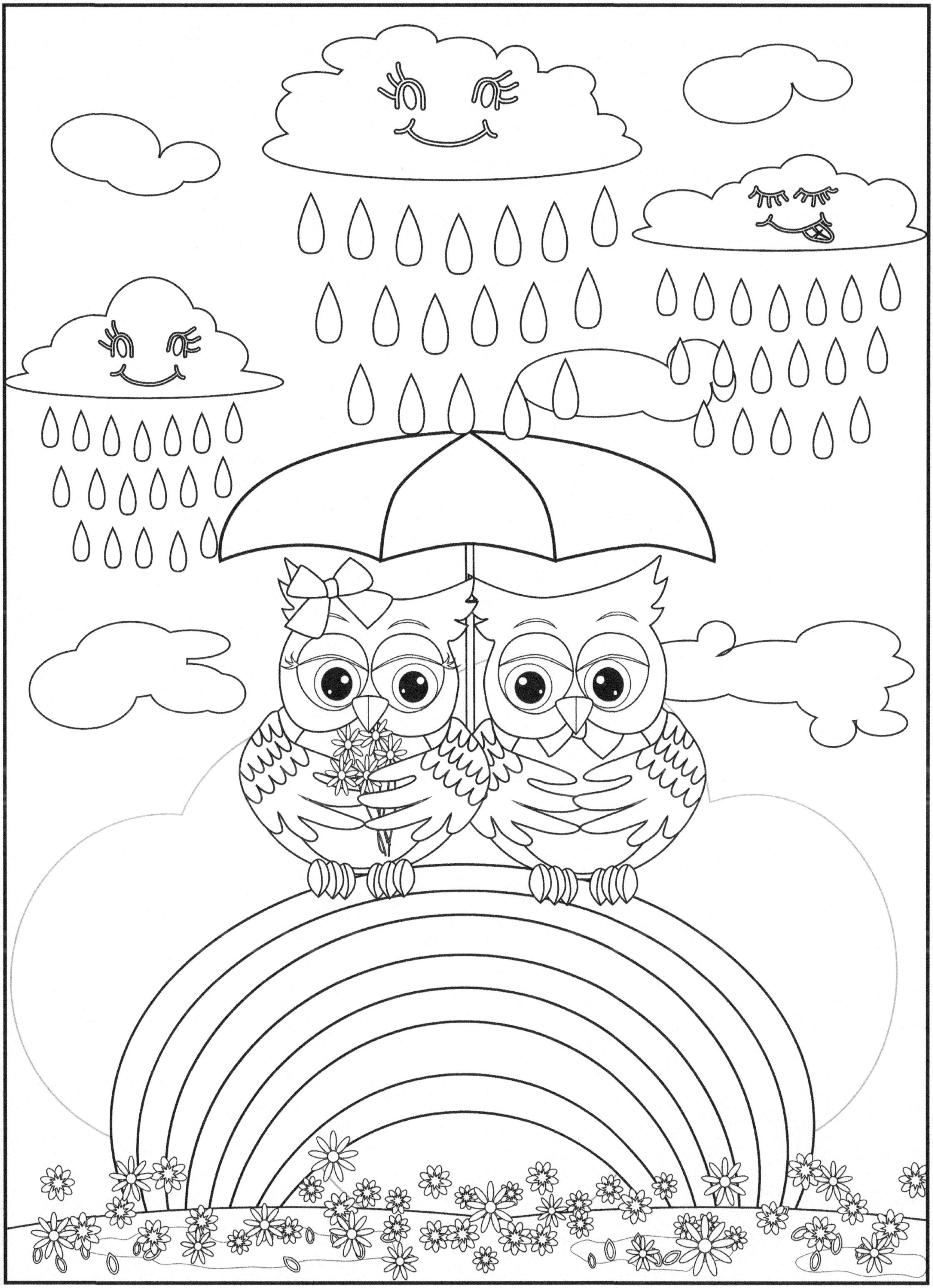

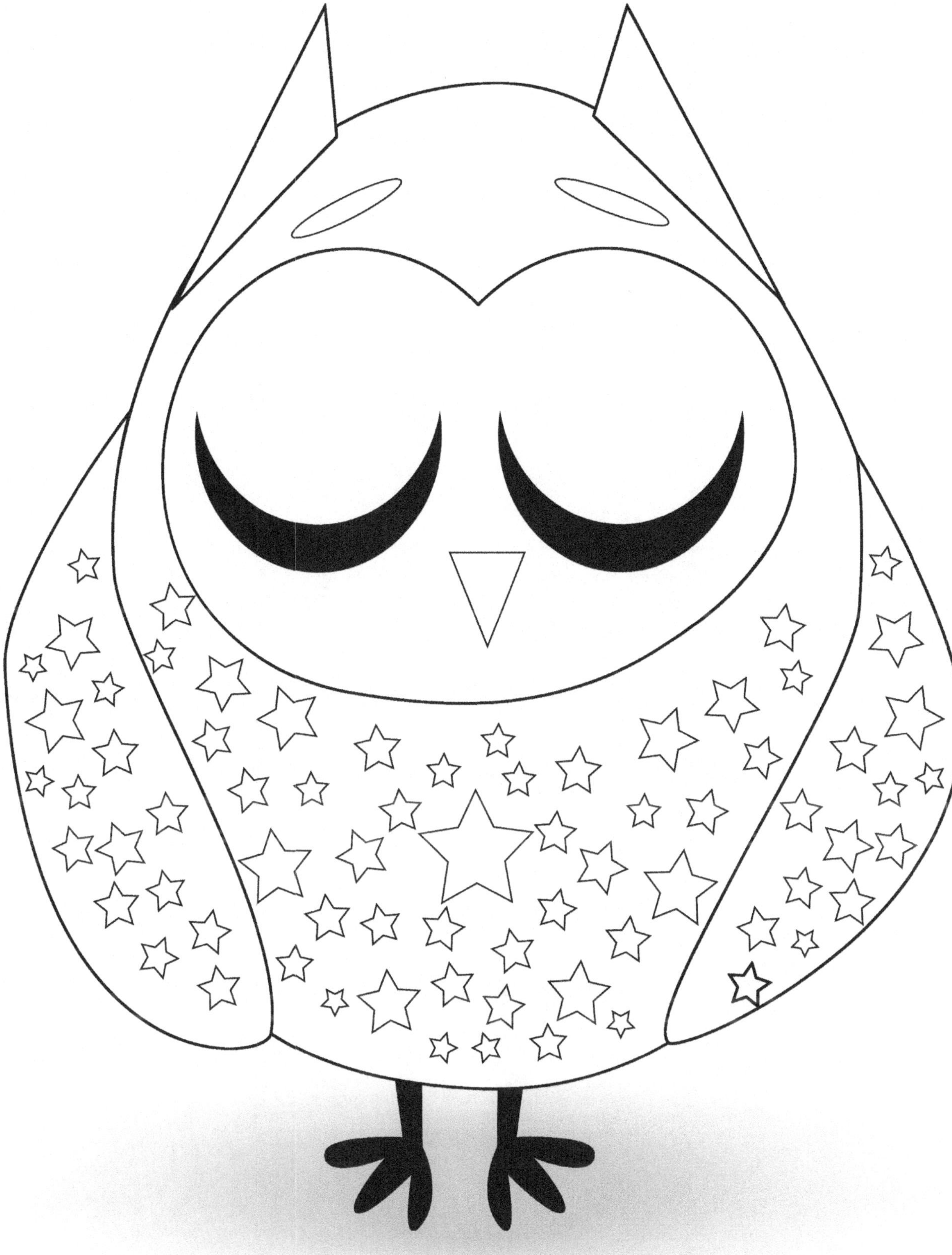

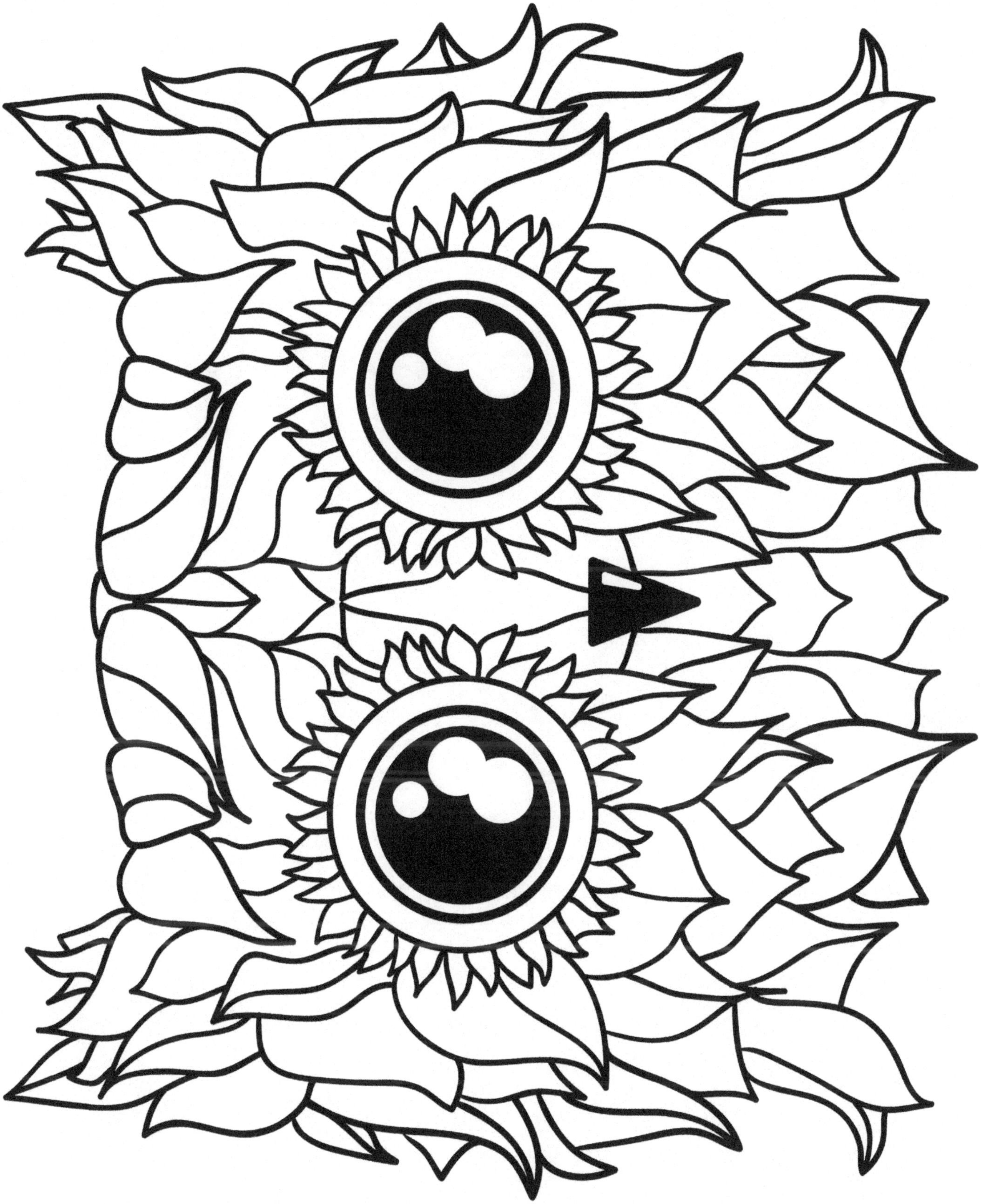

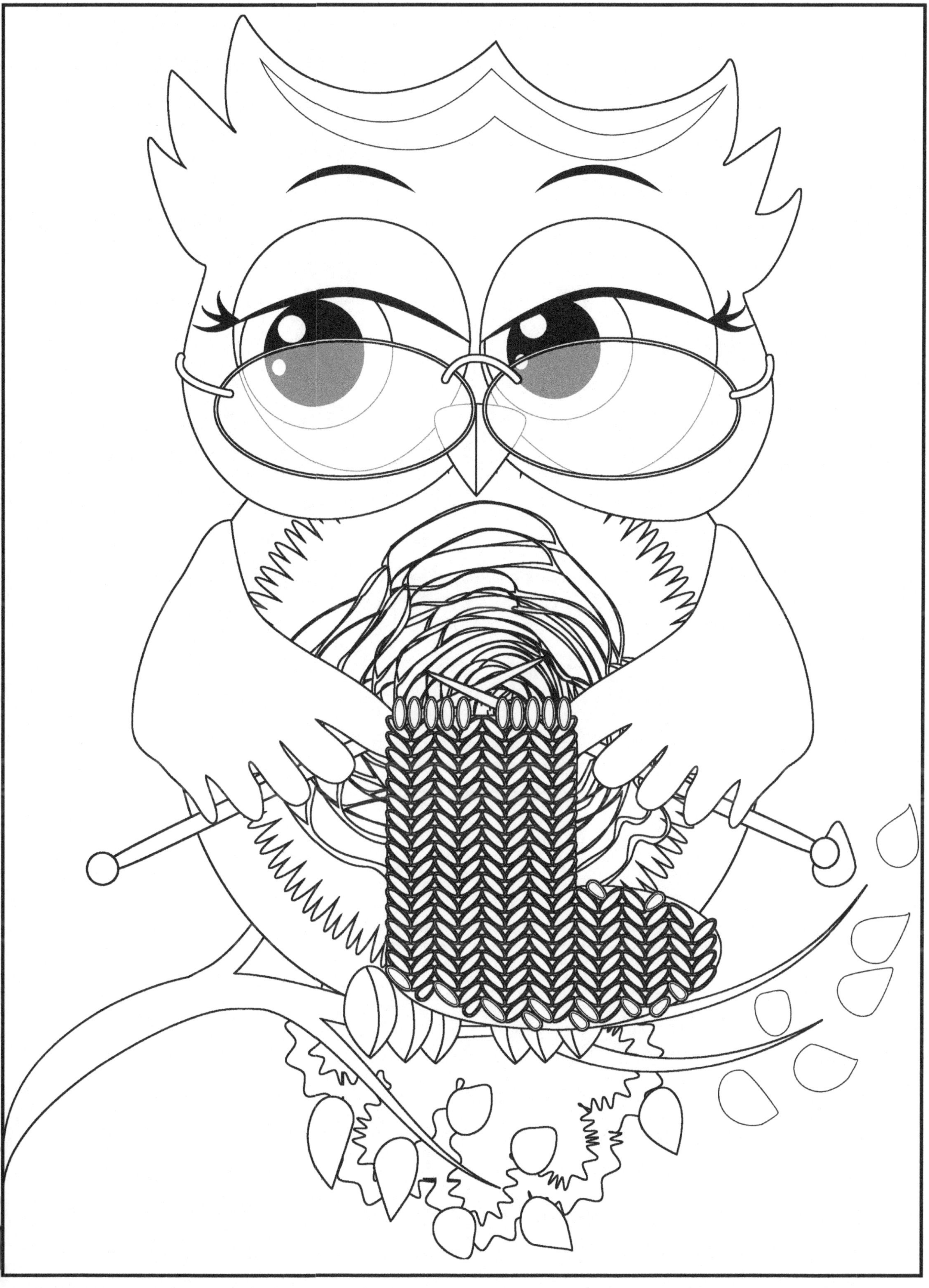

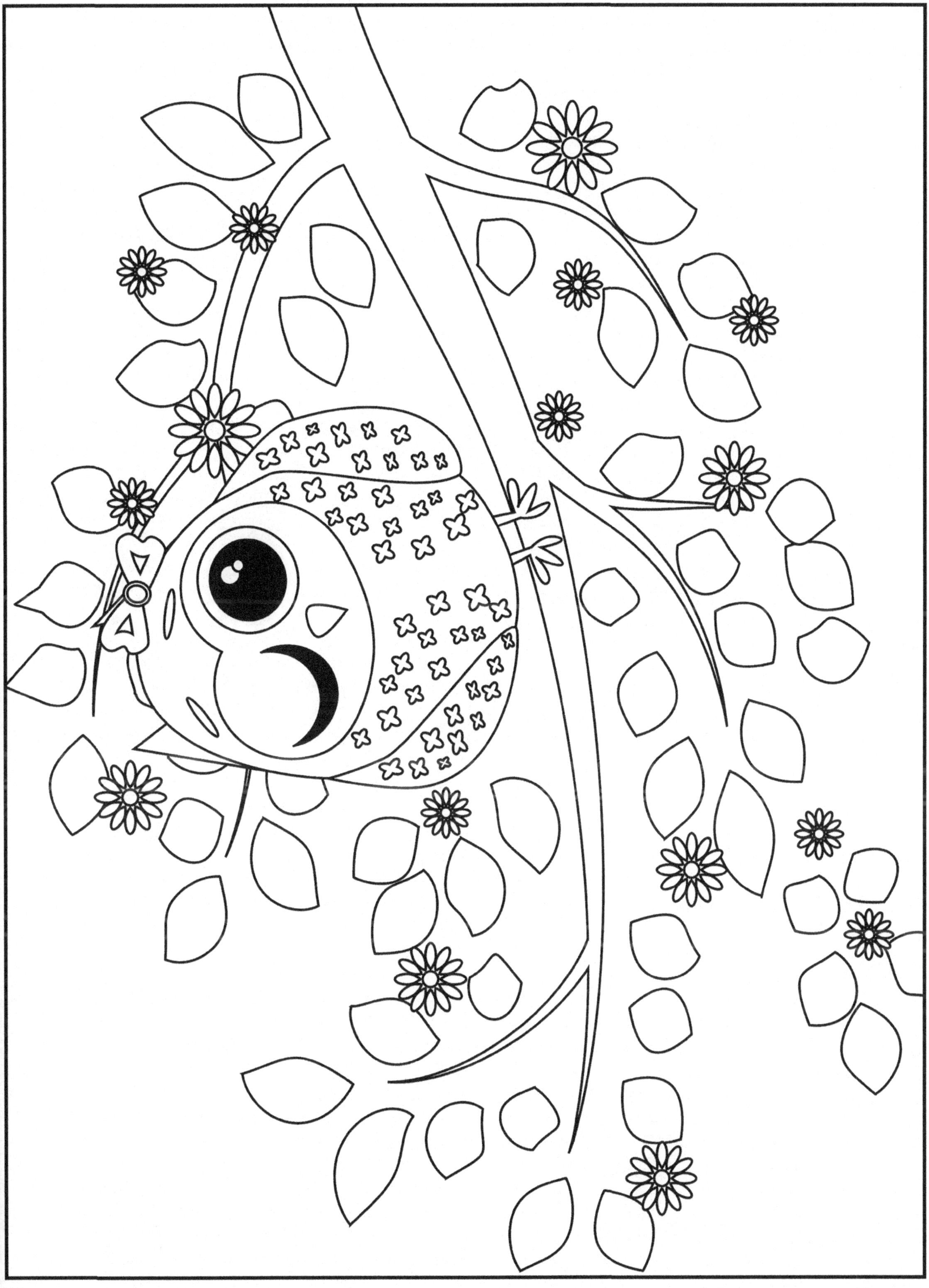

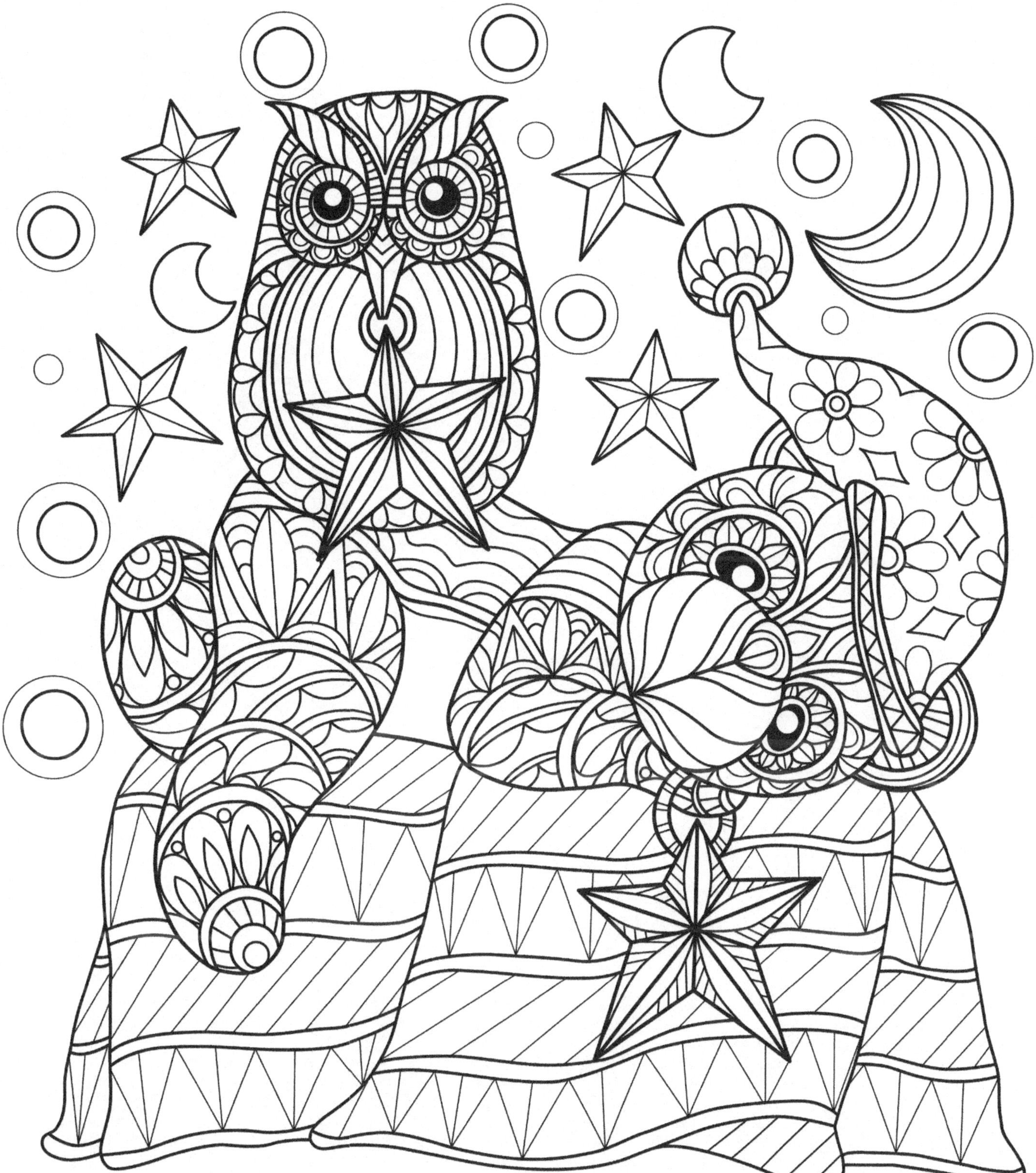

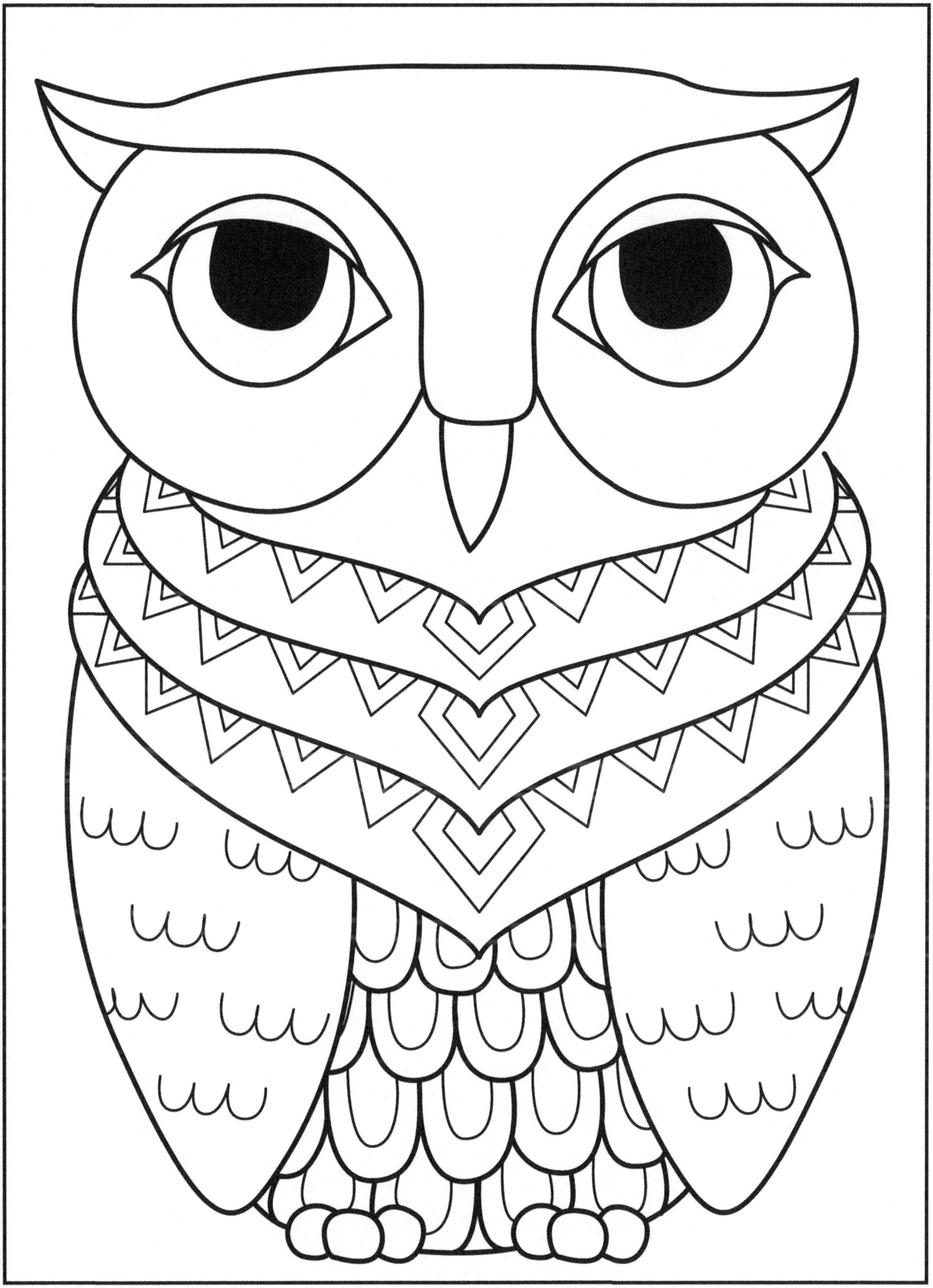

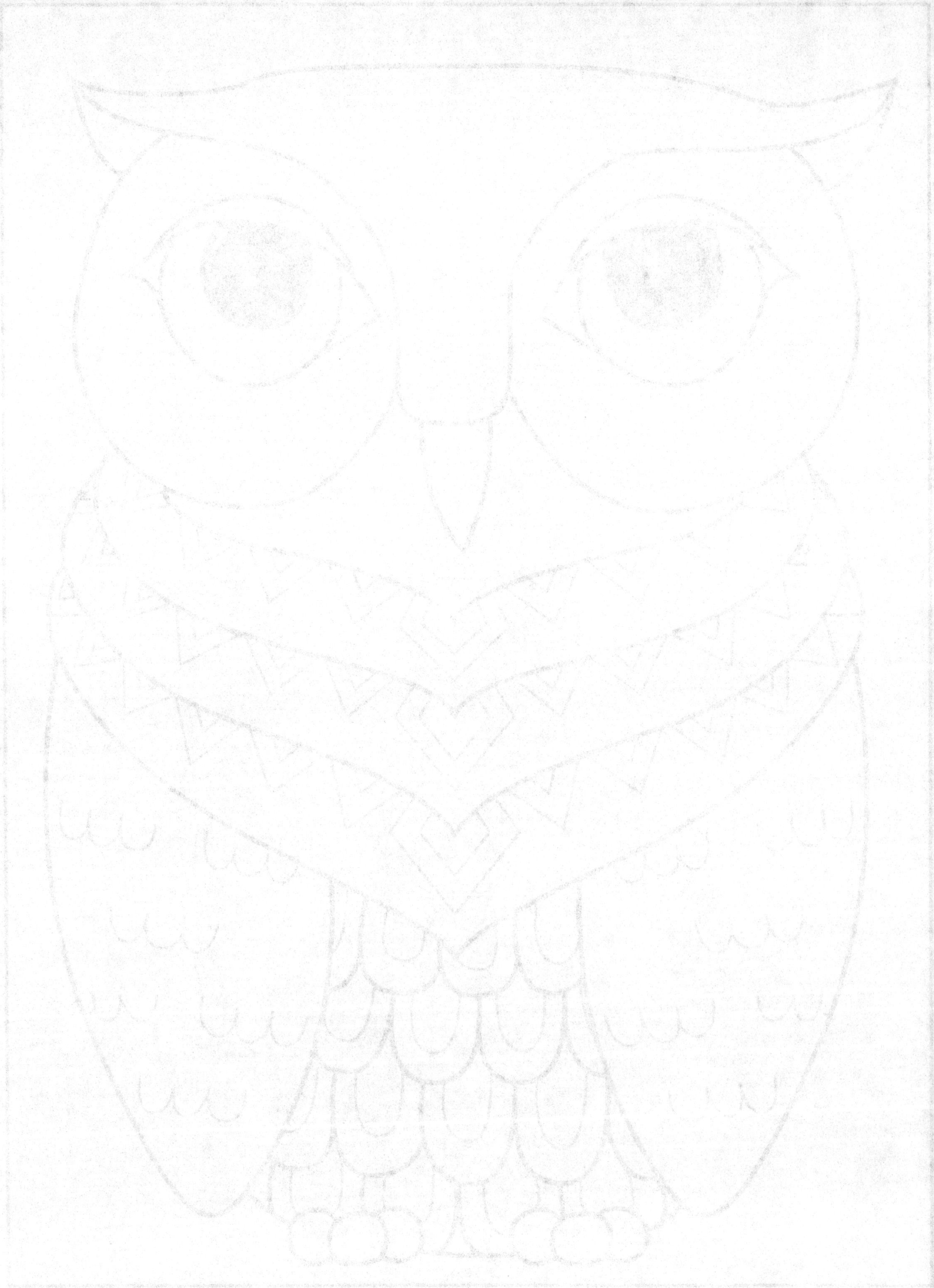

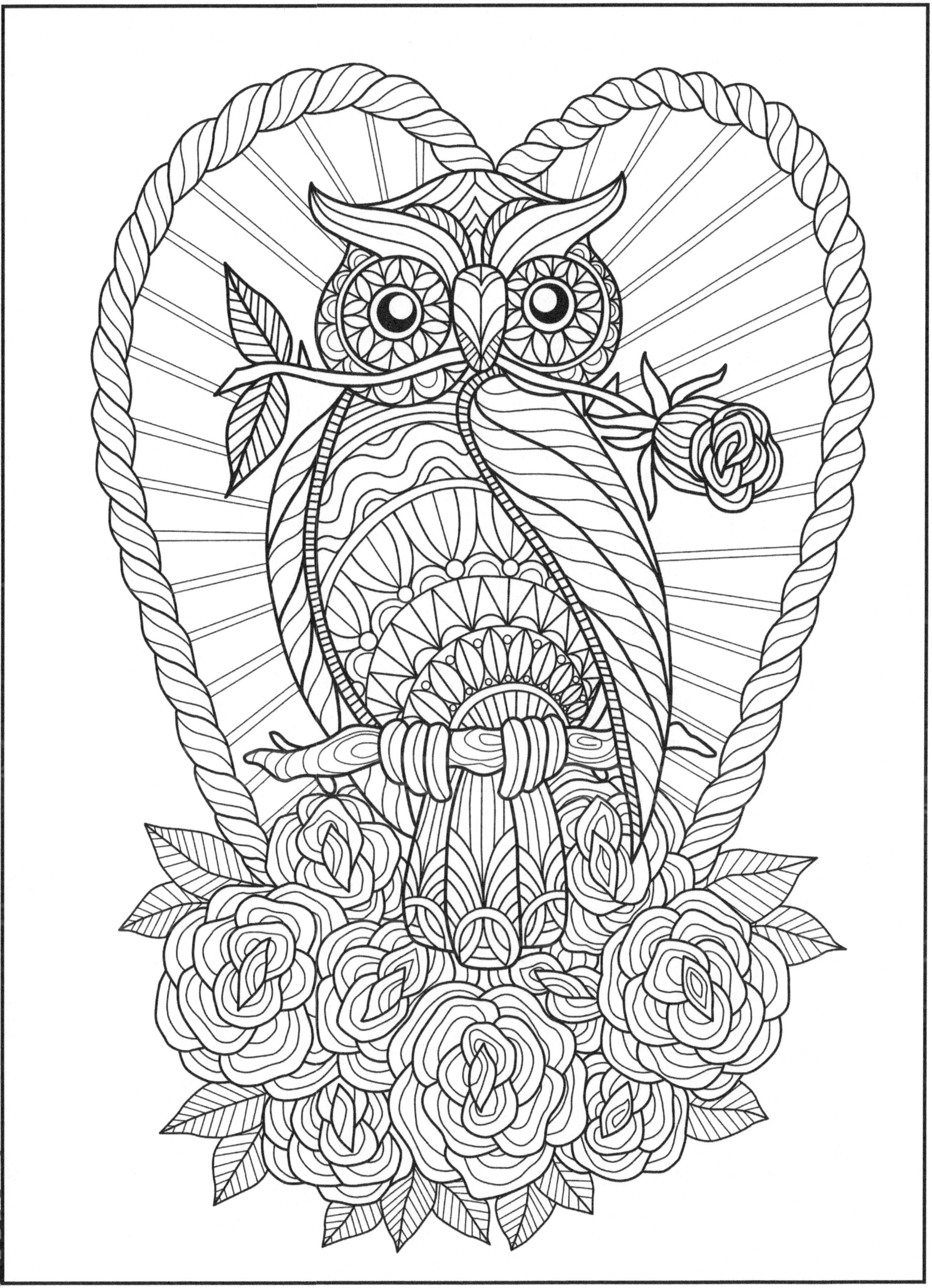

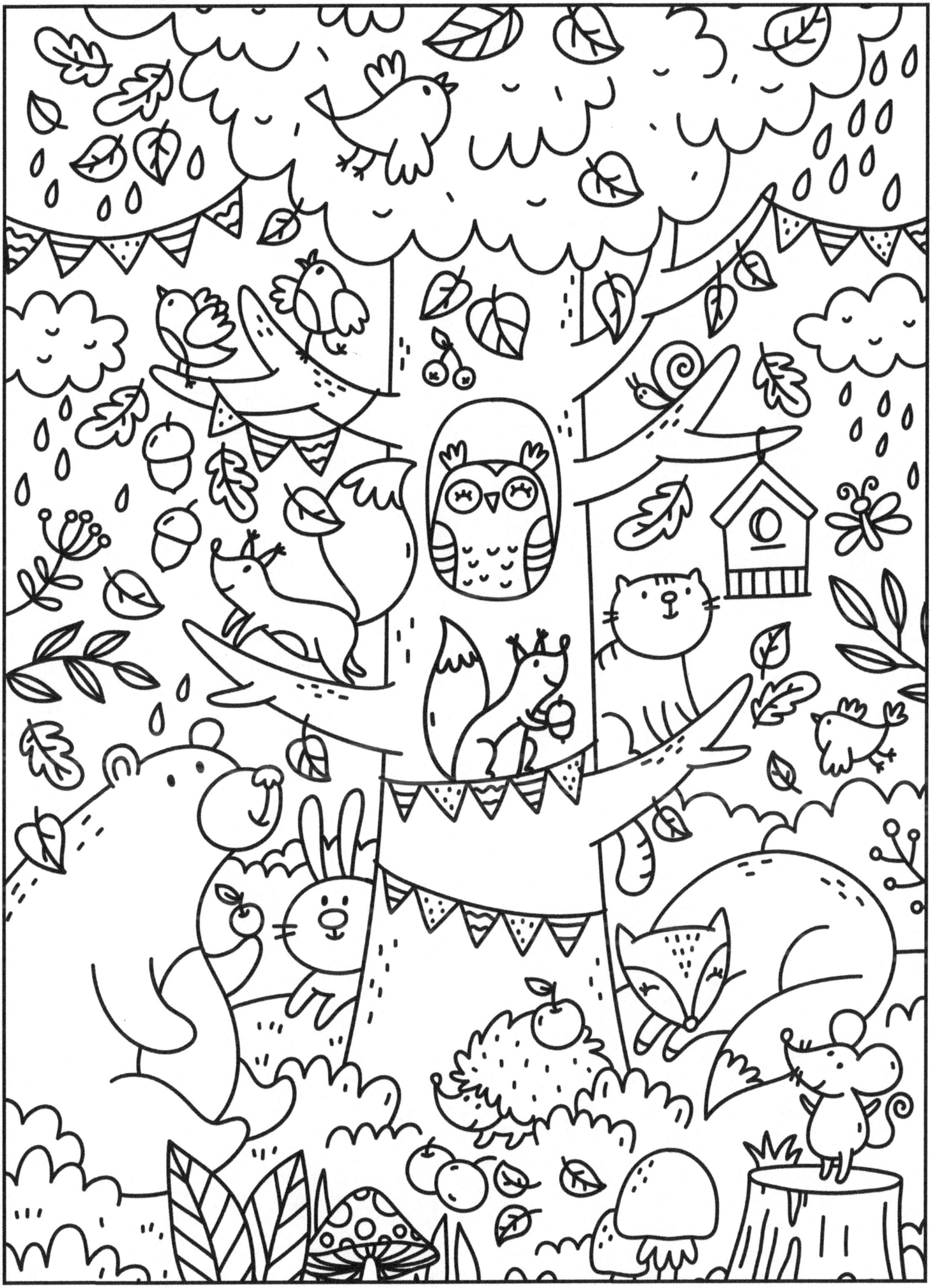

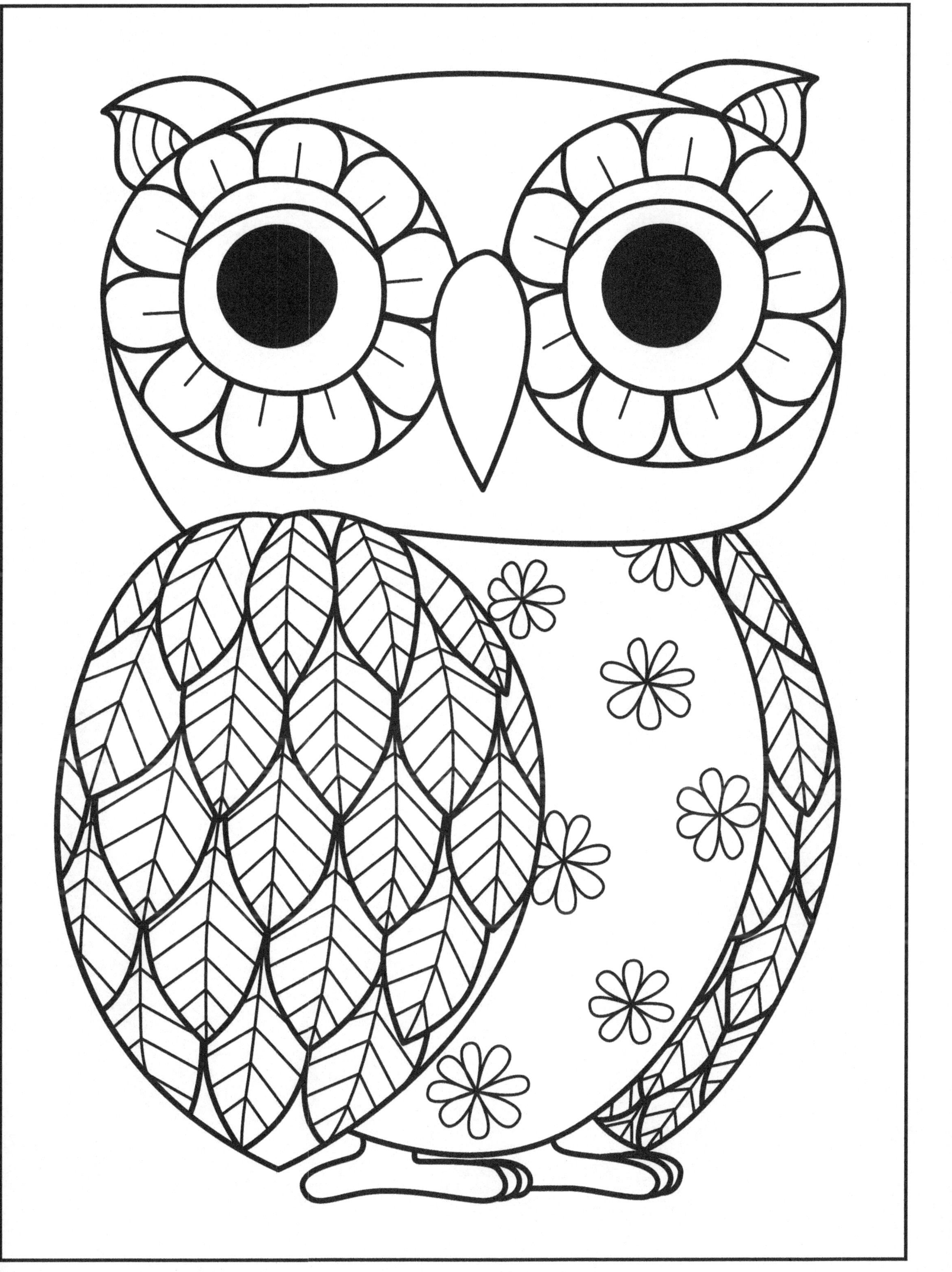

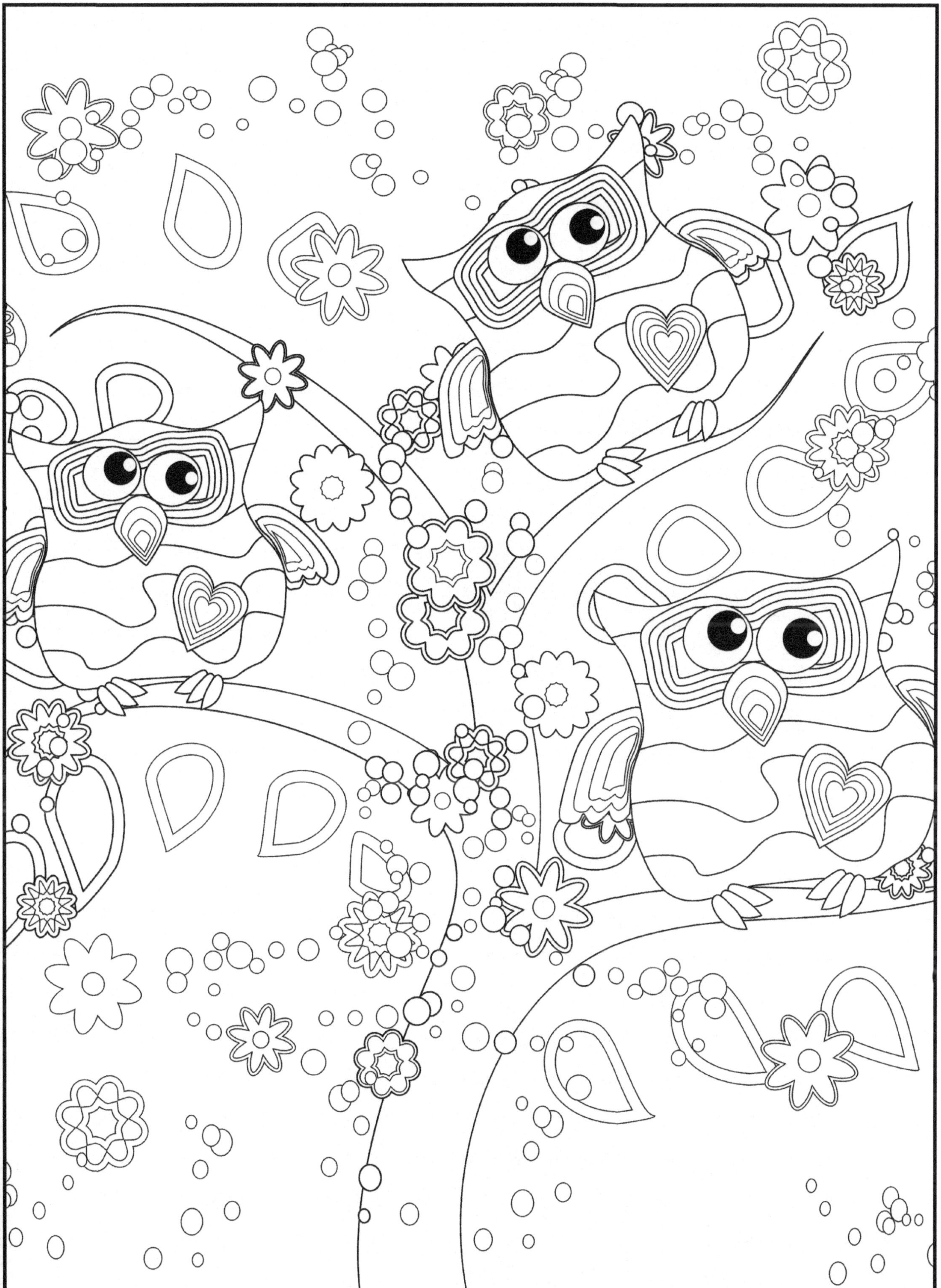

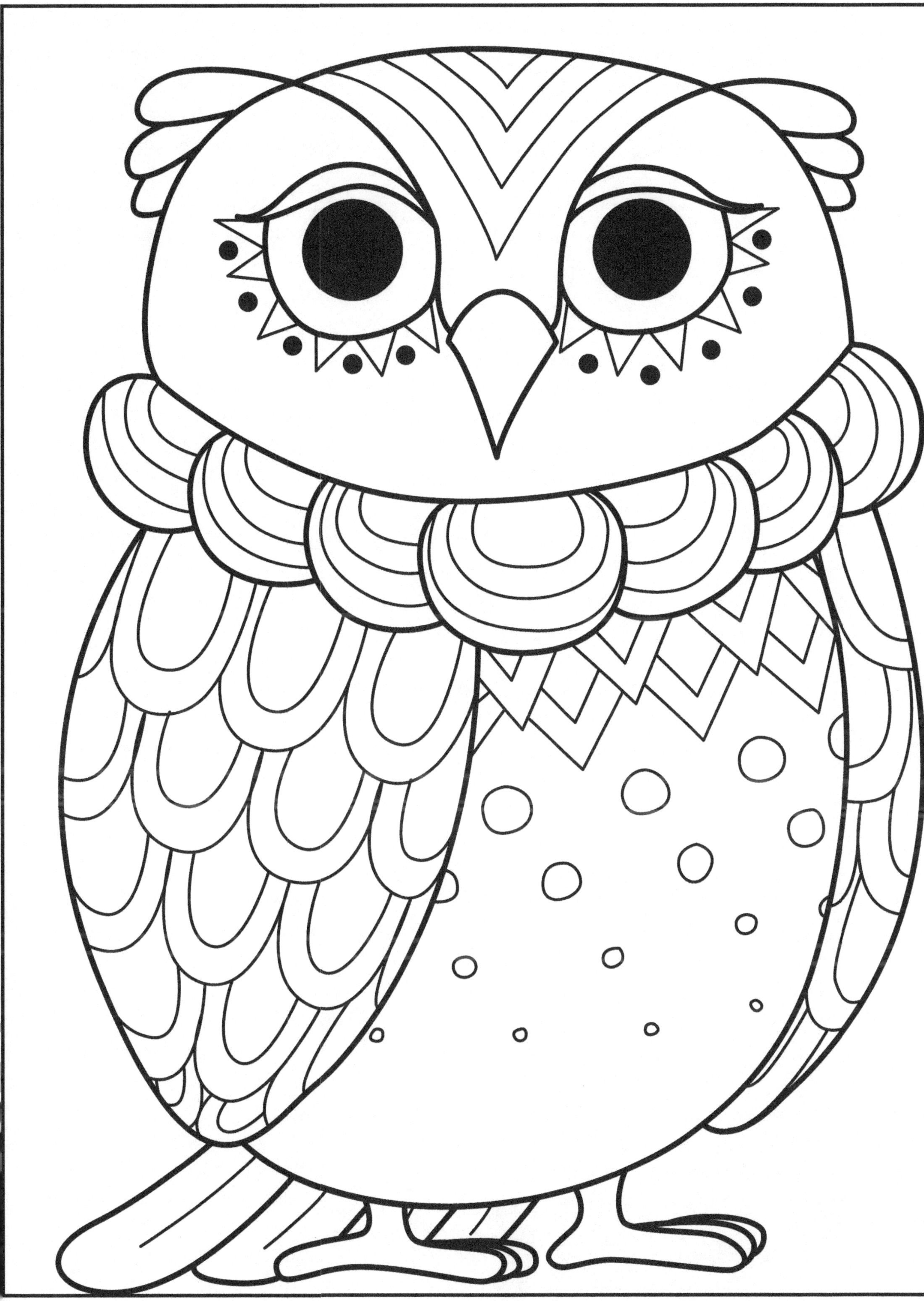

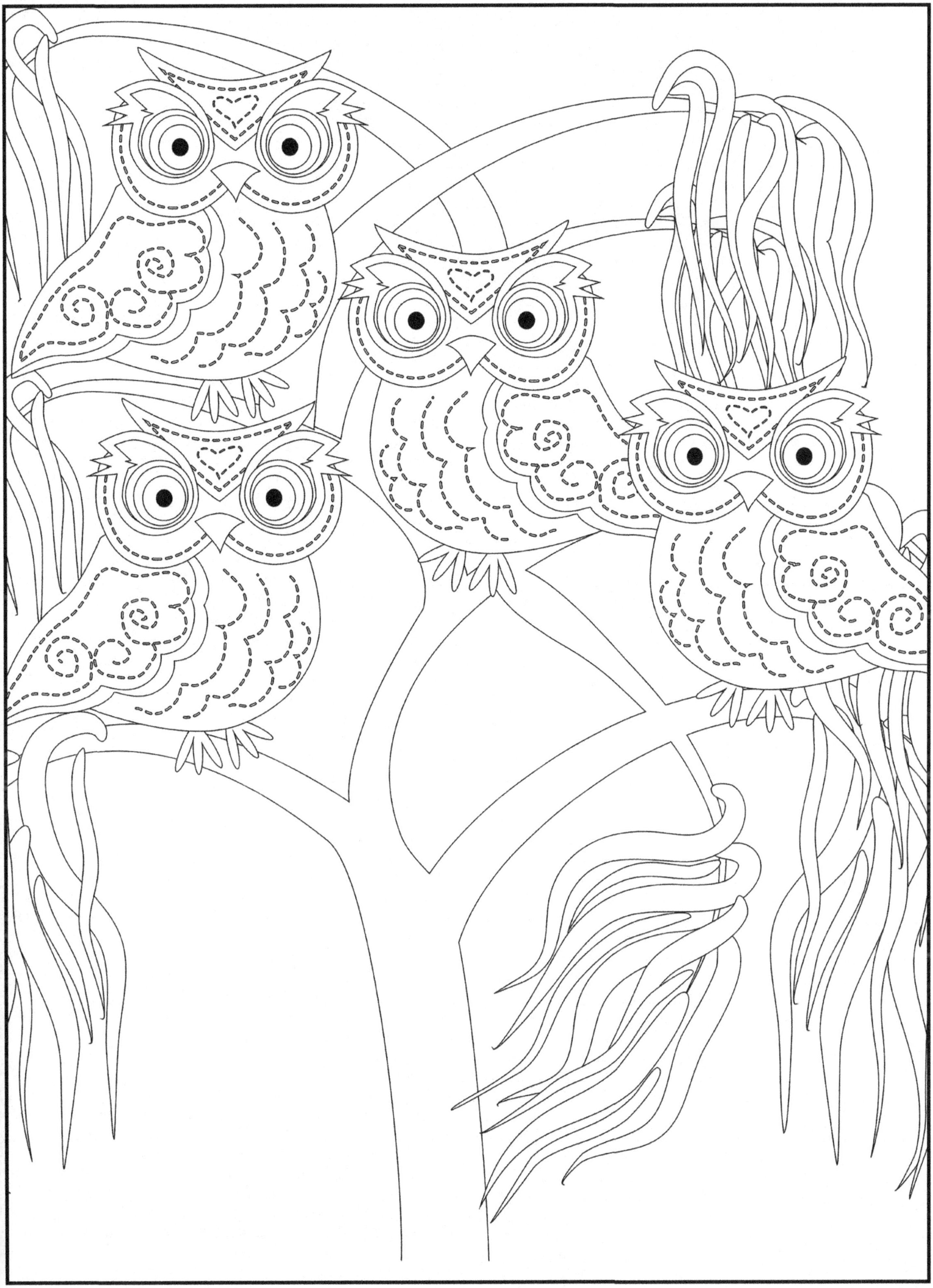

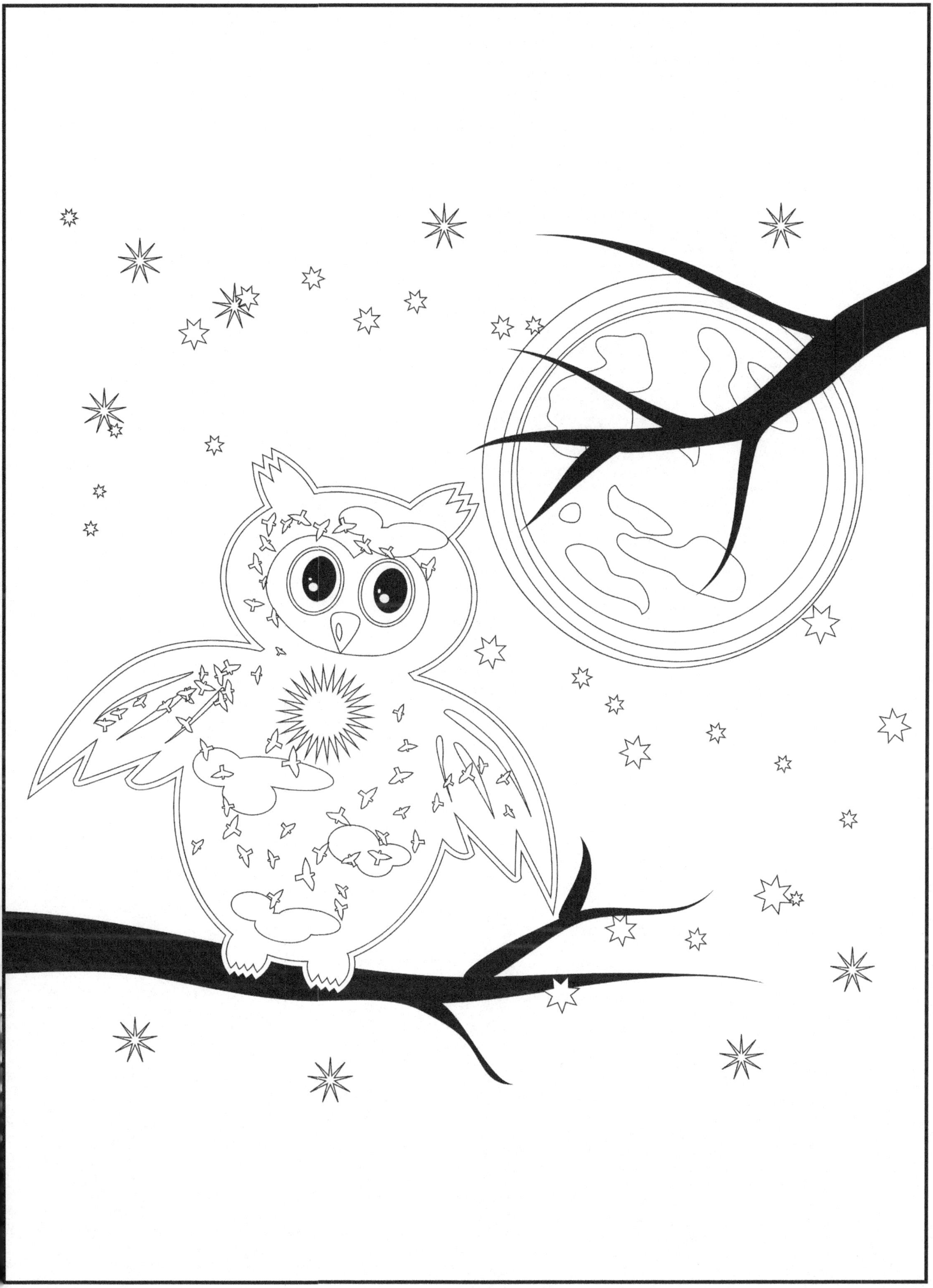

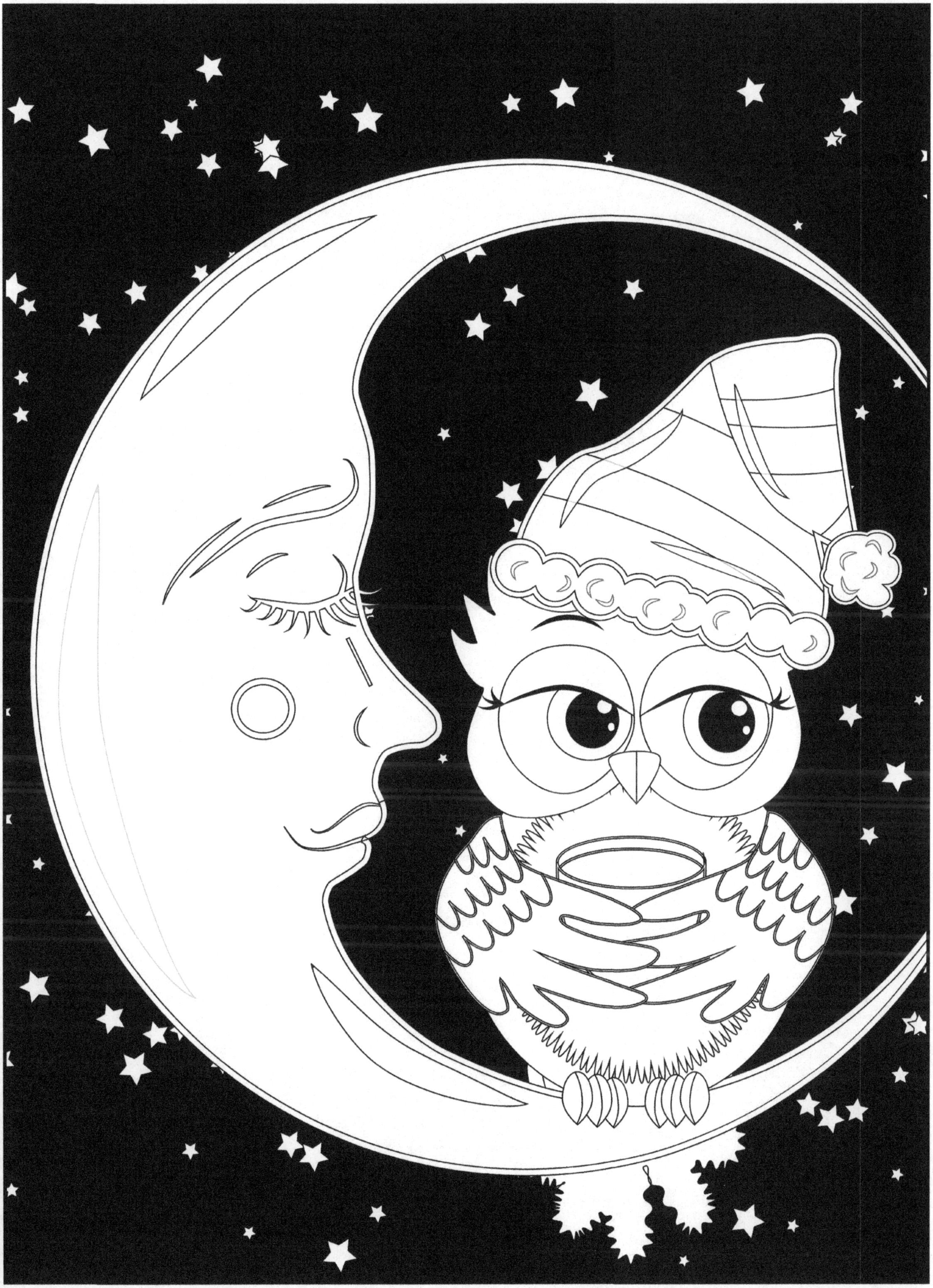

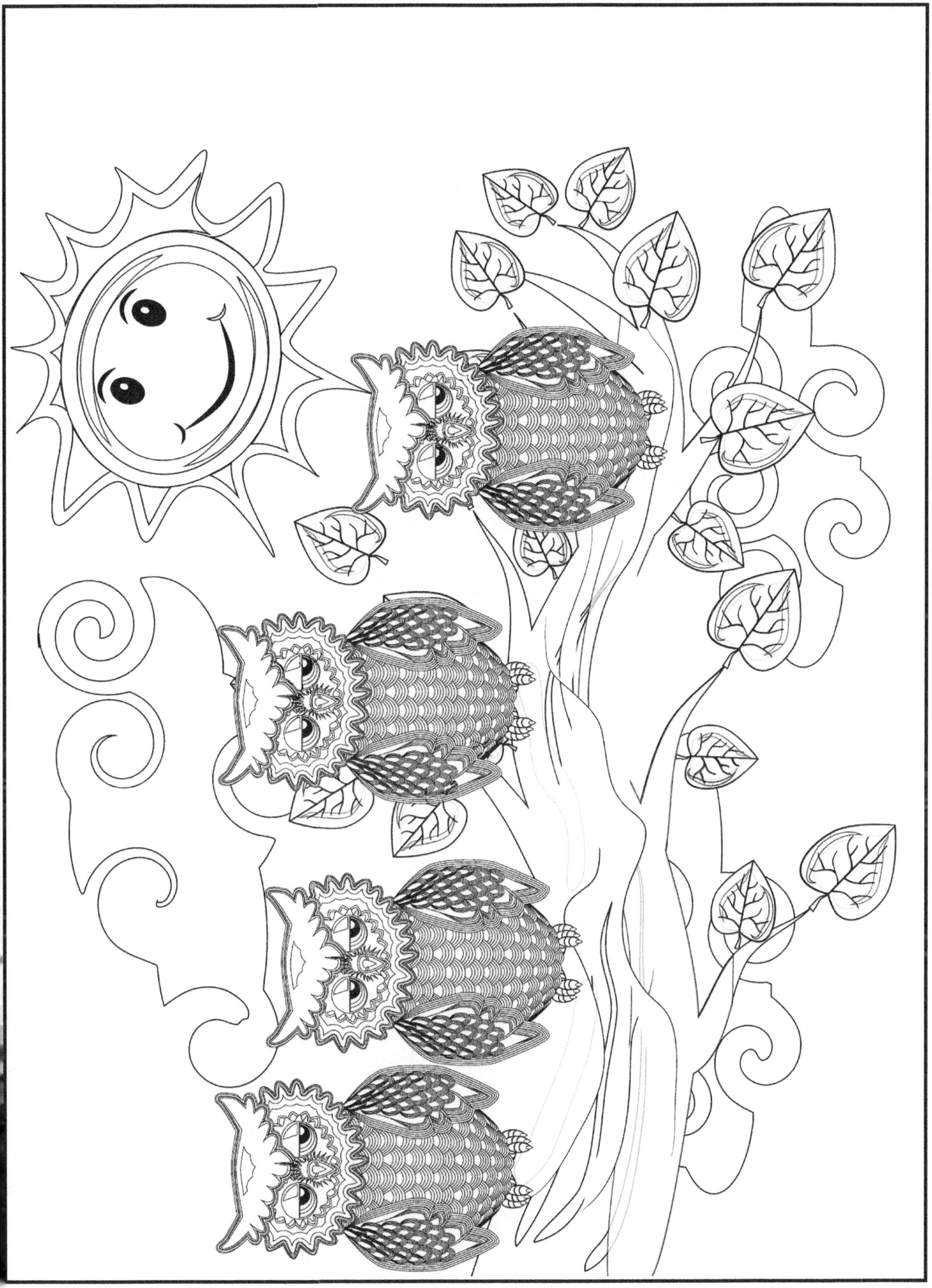

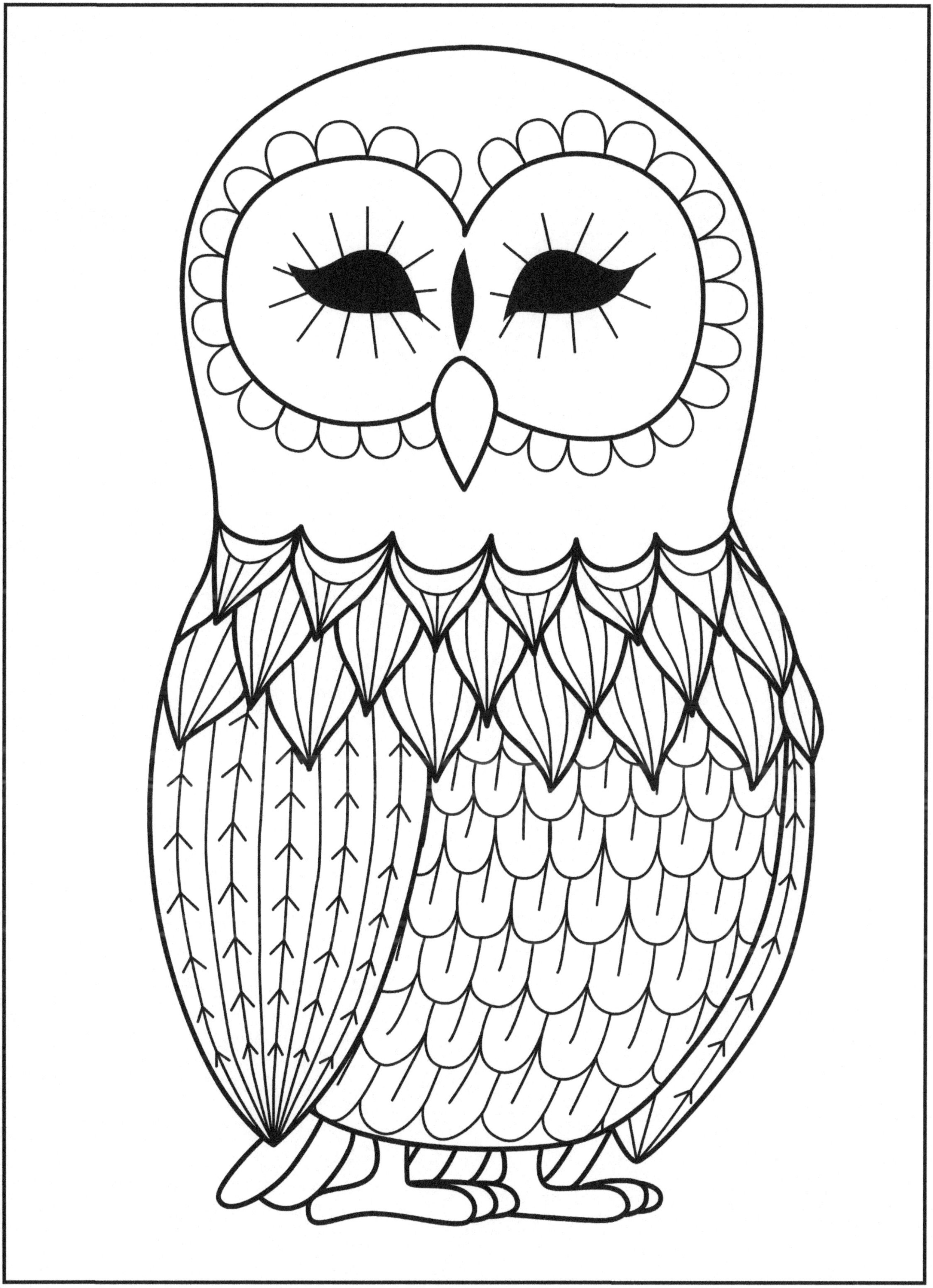

Made in the USA
Las Vegas, NV
14 August 2023

76091365R10052